Tipbook Keyboard & Digital Piano

Publishing Details

This first edition published April 2004 by
The Tipbook Company bv, The Netherlands.

Distributed exclusively by the Hal Leonard Corporation,
7777 West Bluemound Road, P.O. Box 13819,
Milwaukee, Wisconsin 53213.

Typeset in Glasgow and Minion.

Printed in The Netherlands by Hentenaar Boek bv, Nieuwegein.

© 2004 THE TIPBOOK COMPANY BV

144pp

ISBN 90-76192-31-6

Hugo Pinksterboer

Tipbook
Keyboard
& Digital Piano

Handy, clearly written, and up-to-date.
The reference for both beginning and advanced
keyboardists, including Tipcodes and a glossary.

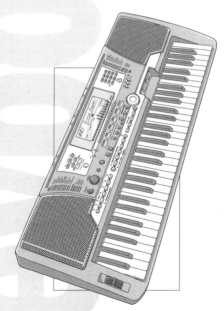

THE **TIPBOOK**
COMPANY

THE BEST GUIDE TO YOUR INSTRUMENT!

Thanks

For their information, their expertise, their time, and their help we'd like to thank the following keyboard and digital piano experts: Eddy Dieters and Joost van Leeuwen, Allard Krijger and Eppo Schaap (*Interface*), Luc Wäckerlin, Nathan Cairo, Kim Burton, Leon Padmos (M-Works), Dick Barten, Aard van Asseldonk (Generalmusic), Rick Oldersom and Michel Lamine, André Rietveld (Yamaha Music), Christian Scheck and Kristof Mertens (Roland Benelux), Carin Tielen, Matthieu Vermeulen, and Nick Zwart.

Anything missing?

Any omissions? Any areas that could be improved? Please go to www.tipbook.com to contact us. Thanks!

The makers

Journalist, writer, and musician **Hugo Pinksterboer**, author of The Tipbook Series, has published hundreds of interviews, articles, and instrument, video, CD, and book reviews for national and international music magazines.

Illustrator, designer, and musician **Gijs Bierenbroodspot** has worked as an art director for a wide variety of magazines and developed numerous ad campaigns. While searching for information about saxophone mouthpieces, he got the idea for this series of books on music and musical instruments. He is responsible for the layout and illustrations of all of the Tipbooks.

Acknowledgements

Concept, design, and illustrations: Gijs Bierenbroodspot

Cover photo: René Vervloet

Editor & proofreader: Robert L. Doerschuk

IN BRIEF

Have you just started playing? Are you thinking of buying a keyboard or a digital piano, or do you want to learn more about the instrument you already have? If so, this book will tell you all you need to know: the main features and characteristics of these instruments; choosing and play-testing keyboards and digital pianos; judging sound; MIDI and other connections; the history and family of the piano and the keyboard – and much more.

The best you can
Having read this Tipbook, you'll be able to decide which instrument is best for you, know how to get the most out of it, and easily grasp any other literature on the subject, from magazines to books and Internet publications.

Begin at the beginning
If you have just started playing, or haven't yet begun, pay particular attention to the first four chapters. Have you been playing longer? Then skip ahead to Chapter 5. Please note that all prices mentioned in this book are based on estimated street prices in US dollars.

Glossary
The glossary at the end of the book briefly explains most of the terms you'll come across as a keyboard player. To make life even easier, it doubles as an index.

Hugo Pinksterboer

CONTENTS

SEE WHAT YOU READ WITH TIPCODE

www.tipbook.com

In addition to numerous illustrations, Tipbooks offer you a new way to see – and even hear – what you are reading about. The Tipcodes that you will come across throughout this book give you access to short movies and soundtracks at www.tipbook.com.

Here is how it works: On page 73 of this book there's a paragraph on synthesizer and pad sounds. Right above that paragraph it says **Tipcode KEYS-016**. Type in that code on the Tipcode page at www.tipbook.com, and you'll hear what some of these sounds sound like. Similar audio examples are available on a variety of subjects; other Tipcodes will display a short movie.

Enter code, watch movie

You enter the Tipcode below the movie window on the Tipcode page. In most cases, you will then see the relevant images or hear a soundtrack within five to ten seconds.

Quick start

The movies, photo series, and soundtracks are designed so that they start quickly. If you miss something the first time, you can of course repeat them. And if it all happens too fast, use the pause button below the movie window.

Plug-ins

If the software you need to view the movies or photos is not yet installed on your computer, you'll automatically be told what you need, and where you can download it. This kind of software (*plug-ins*) is free.

First, make your selection: Tipcode, chords and fingering charts, or the glossary.

The Tipcode window displays movies, photo series, fingering charts, chords, and explanations of the words used in this book.

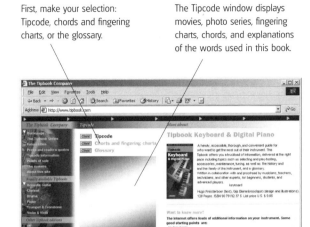

Enter a Tipcode here and click on the button. Want to see it again? Click again.

These buttons and links take you directly to other interesting sites.

Tipcodes listed

For your convenience, the Tipcodes used in this book are shown in a single list on page 132.

Still more at www.tipbook.com

You can find even more information at www.tipbook.com. For instance, you can look up words in the glossaries of all the Tipbooks published to date. For guitarists and pianists there are chord diagrams; and for saxophonists, clarinetists, and flutists there are fingering charts; for drummers there are the rudiments. Also included are links to some of the websites mentioned in the *Want to Know More?* section of each Tipbook.

1. A KEYBOARD PLAYER?

As a keyboard player, you play one of the most versatile instruments around – whether it is a digital piano, a home keyboard, or any other instrument with black and white keys. You can play solo or in a band. You can play almost any style of music. And you can hook up your instrument up to other instruments, or you can connect it to a computer and use the computer as a recording studio or an interactive tutor...

This chapter mainly looks at what you can do with a *keyboard* or a *digital piano*. If you're not sure which instrument of the two you should get, this should help you choose.

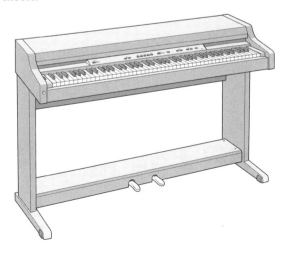

Digital pianos usually offer fewer sounds and features than keyboards.

Pianist

If you would like to play the piano, you may prefer a digital piano to a traditional, acoustic piano. Why? A digital piano allows you to practice without bothering your neighbors or housemates, it doesn't need to be tuned, it hardly needs maintenance, and it's often less expensive.

Keyboardist

If you like to have easy access to the sounds of a hundred or more different instruments, from organs to guitars and from flutes to saxophones, and if you want to be able to produce the sound of a full band while playing just by yourself, you're better off with a keyboard, also known as *portable keyboard* or *home keyboard*.

Solo

Both pianos and keyboards are great solo instruments: You can play all by yourself in a wide variety of styles. That said, keyboards are less often used in jazz and classical music; pianos are better suited for those styles.

Automatic orchestra

If you want to play solo, a keyboard can provide you with a complete automatic orchestra with a bassist, a drummer, strings, a guitarist or a pianist, and other instruments. The orchestra follows you as you play. With a keyboard, you are a one-man band in the true sense of the word.

Practice partner

This *automatic accompaniment* feature also turns the keyboard into a great practice partner: You can rehearse your parts at home while the instrument replaces your band.

A keyboard has numerous sounds and a built-in band – the automatic accompaniment – that can play various styles of music.

In a band

You can use a keyboard in a band too. Just switch off the automatic accompaniment and use the instrument to play a piano part, string harmonies, flute melodies, a guitar solo, or whatever else you like.

Synthesizer

However, if you play in a band, a *synthesizer* may be more suitable. Synthesizers don't have automatic accompaniment (you don't need that in a band), but they allow you to create and play a wider variety of sounds than most keyboards do. There's more on synthesizers in Chapter 12.

Any style

From jazz to techno, from country to Latin, from classical to ethnic music, up-to-date keyboards provide you with accompaniments in the latest musical styles – and a growing number of instruments can be updated through the Internet.

New songs

Keyboard instruments are very often used by composers in any style of music. If you write your music on a home keyboard or digital piano, you can use its built-in recorder to play a new song to your band members, giving them an idea of what it should sound like. Or you can connect your instrument to your computer and have it print your composition, for example.

More

There are many more things that make pianos and keyboard very attractive instruments. Some examples?

- On keyboards and pianos, every note has **its own key**. You want a higher note? Move to the right. Want a lower one? Move to the left. That's about as easy as it can be.
- Learning to play a keyboard instrument well takes just as long as learning any other instrument. But it **won't take you that long** to play something that sounds acceptable. On a keyboard you may produce something quite impressive sounding within just a few weeks.
- A growing number of instruments features an **onboard 'tutor'** that helps you learn to play the instrument more easily.

- Keyboards start at **very friendly prices**, and digital pianos are generally cheaper than acoustic ones.
- Most electronic keyboard instruments have **built-in amplification**, so there's no need to buy them as extras. A headphone socket is a standard feature on all of them.

Any time, day or night...

Keyboard?

The word 'keyboard' is a bit confusing. Originally, it indicates the range of black and white keys that you find on pianos, organs, and synthesizers. These are all *keyboard instruments*. Someone who plays 'keys' plays a keyboard instrument.

Keyboard

Later on, 'keyboard' grew to be short for home keyboard or portable keyboard, two terms that seem to be used interchangeably. It adds to the confusion that 'keyboard' is sometimes used to indicate synthesizers or other keyboard instruments as well.

Keyboards!

Mastering one keyboard instrument gives you easy access to most other keyboard instruments: After all, the layout of the keys is the same on each one. Though different keyboard instruments require very different playing techniques, there are many keyboard players who play them all. After all, it's not that unusual to see a band with someone who uses a digital piano, a synthesizer, or even more keyboard instruments in one setup!

2. QUICK TOUR

Keyboards often look quite intimidating, with lots of buttons, knobs, sliders, and other controls. Most digital pianos are easier on the eye. Here's a quick tour to take the mystery out of both.

First, the keys that make up the keyboard or *manual*. If you take a closer look, you will see that the keys are divided into alternate groups of two and three black keys. This grouping makes all the notes very easy to find.

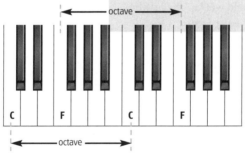

... alternate groups of two and three black keys.

The C and the F   Tipcode KEYS-001
Two examples? The white key just before *two* black keys always gives the note C. And the white key just before a group of *three* black keys gives the note F.

Octave
There are always eight white keys from one C to the next. Such a group of eight is called an *octave*. Within each octave you will also find five black keys.

Seven octaves

Acoustic pianos and most digital pianos have 88 keys. This adds up to a little more than seven octaves. With these 88 keys you can play lower notes than a bass, and higher notes than a piccolo, the very smallest flute.

Fewer keys

Most home keyboards or portable keyboards have fewer keys. If you're serious about playing, then go for one with at least 61 keys (*i.e.*, five octaves).

Samples

When you play the keys of a keyboard or a digital piano, you are actually playing back digital recordings. These recordings, *samples*, are stored in the instrument's memory. There is a series of samples for every type of sound: one series for the grand piano sound, one for the rock organ sound, and so on.

Loud and soft

Most keyboards and all pianos have *touch sensitive* keyboards: The harder you play a key, the louder the sound will be. The instrument's overall volume is set with a *volume control.*

DIGITAL PIANOS

Digital pianos are often used instead of an acoustic piano. When you play the keys of an acoustic piano, you make a series of felt hammers hit the piano's strings. This gives the keys a certain feel. Good digital pianos mimic this feel, usually by incorporating small hammers in the instrument's mechanism or *action.*

Other instruments   Tipcode KEYS-002

To make a digital piano sound like an acoustic one, all the notes of an acoustic piano have been recorded (sampled). These samples are stored in the digital piano's memory. Most digital pianos have samples of other instruments as well. Usually there are a few different types of pianos, some electric pianos, a couple of organs, and a harpsichord. Some non-keyboard sounds are often included too, such as strings or a choir.

Different types

Digital pianos generally come in three different designs: the ones that look like small upright pianos, either with or without a full cabinet below the keyboard; the ones that look like a (baby) grand piano (see page 46); and the so-called *stage pianos* or *portable pianos*, which usually don't have speakers.

A stage piano.

KEYBOARDS

In effect, a keyboard is a band-in-a-box, with an onboard drummer, a bass player, a string section (*e.g.*, violinists), and a host of other electronic 'musicians.' Just press the *start* button, hit a key with your left hand, and the orchestra starts playing in the style you have selected: rock, waltz, jazz, hard-core, country, techno, dance – you name it.

Sounds

Home keyboards or portable keyboards usually have anywhere from a hundred to more than a thousand *sounds*, *tones* or *voices* to choose from: organs, electric and acoustic guitars, basses, violins, cellos, saxophones, flutes, trombones, basses, drums, cowbells, vocals, ethnic instruments, synthesizer sounds, sound effects (applause, gunshots), and much more.

Keyboard or piano?

Each keyboard has a number of piano sounds too. So why bother buying a digital piano? Because its action is closer to that of an acoustic piano, the range of its keyboard is bigger, and because most digital pianos sound more like their acoustic relatives.

The keyboard

The keyboard is a descendant of the organ, and its keys feel like organ keys. They require less finger strength than piano-type keys do, so they're easier to play. But if you want to learn to play the piano, you're much better off with a digital piano featuring a piano-like *hammer action*.

Chords

The only way to play chords (three or more notes at a time) on a piano is to actually hit all the right notes. On keyboards, you can play chords using just one or two fingers: Keyboards have a *chord recognition* system.

Automatic accompaniment

The automatic accompaniment section of a keyboard is like a virtual band. Once you press the *start* button, the band will follow the chords you play. The only thing you have to do first is tell the band whether it should play jazz, rock, Latin, or any other style.

Intros and endings   Tipcode KEYS-003

Many songs start with an intro. Press the *intro* button, and the instrument will play an introduction that fits the style of music you have selected. Likewise, keyboards feature one or more *endings* for the available styles.

Variations and fills   Tipcode KEYS-004

A button marked *variation* produces a slightly different accompaniment pattern, which you can use in the chorus of a song, for example; for the next verse, you may go back to the *main* or *basic pattern*. The *fill* or *fill-in* button produces a short variation, usually including a drum roll of some sort. Fills are often used to mark the beginning of the next section of a song.

Accompaniment controls: start, stop, fill-in, variation... (Roland)

Pianos with auto accompaniments

Some pianos have built-in accompaniments too. Depending on the brand, these instruments are known as *ensemble pianos*, *rhythm pianos*, *intelligent pianos*, or *digital ensembles*, among other names. They offer all the other features of keyboards as well, including a large number of sounds.

COMMON FEATURES

Now that you know the main differences between keyboards and digital pianos, it's time to take a look at some of their common features. The illustrations show where everything is located on a typical instrument.

Demo

Most instruments have a *demo* button. Hitting it will make the instrument play a demonstration of what it can do. Some instruments have a hundred or more demo songs on board. These can also be used to entertain the audience while you're having an intermission!

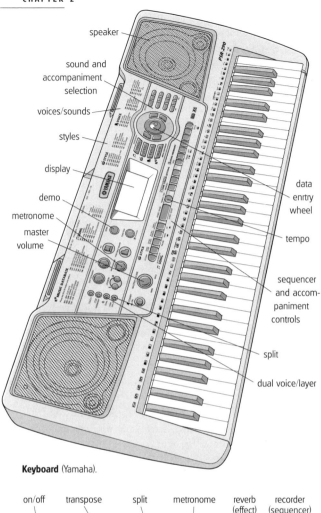

speaker

sound and
accompaniment
selection

voices/sounds

styles

display

demo

metronome

master
volume

data
enrtry
wheel

tempo

sequencer
and accom-
paniment
controls

split

dual voice/layer

Keyboard (Yamaha).

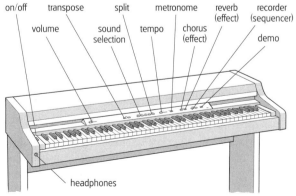

on/off   transpose   split   metronome   reverb   recorder
                                             (effect)   (sequencer)

volume   sound   tempo   chorus   demo
          selection   (effect)

headphones

Digital piano (Yamaha).

Speakers

On keyboards, the *speakers* are often in full view, sitting behind a *speaker grille.* On pianos they're usually hidden. Amplification is taken care of by an onboard *amplifier.*

Display

Keyboards usually have a *display* that shows a lot of information, ranging from the sounds and music style you have selected to the notes and the chords you play, the tempo, the measure you are in, and more. Most pianos have fairly basic displays.

Selecting sounds and styles

Pianos with only a few different sounds usually have a button for each sound. Simply press the button with the sound you are looking for, and start playing. Instruments that feature many different voices have no room for dedicated buttons, of course: You select sounds and styles with either a numeric keypad, by using a combination of buttons, or by making a selection on the instrument's display, for example.

Selecting sounds on a basic digital piano.

Tempo

When you choose a style on a keyboard, the instrument usually selects an appropriate tempo for that style. Of course, you are free to make the band play faster or slower.

Metronome

Most digital pianos have a built-in *metronome* instead: a device that states the tempo with a steady series of clicks or beeps. Metronomes can usually be set in various time signatures (*e.g.,* $\frac{3}{4}$, $\frac{4}{4}$, $\frac{6}{8}$), producing a different sound at the first beat of each bar. Some can play odd time signatures too (*e.g.,* $\frac{5}{4}$).

Metronome controls (left)

Pads

Keyboards often have a special set of pads or keys that can trigger drum sounds, sound effects, guitar riffs, or other sounds that spice up the music. They're commonly known as *multipads*, *touch pads*, *touch keys*, or *session partner pads*.

Bass drums and timbales

On most keyboards you can use the regular keys to play a host of percussion instruments, ranging from bass drums to timbales and congas. Small icons of these instruments are often pictured above or below the keys. You can usually store the rhythms that you create this way.

Split

Want to play a double bass sound with your left hand and a flute with your right? No problem: Most instruments have a *split* feature that divides the keyboard into a lower (left hand) and an upper (right hand) section. You can choose a different instrument for each section.

Layer   Tipcode KEYS-005

If you want to blend, say, the sound of a piano with that of string section, you can do so by simply stacking these sounds on top of each other. This feature is usually called *layer*, *layering*, *dual voice*, or *dual mode*.

Effects

All but the most basic keyboards and pianos offer various effects that enhance the sound by adding warmth and spaciousness, creating echoes, and so on. The two most common effects are *reverb* and *chorus*. Reverb can make it sound as if you play in a big hall or a church, for example. Chorus is an effect that makes instruments sound fuller – as if you hear a choir singing, rather than a single voice.

Pitch bend and modulation   Tipcode KEYS-006

Many digital keyboard instruments have two wheels to the left of the keyboard itself. One is used for *pitch bends*, bending the notes up the way guitarists often do. (On keyboards you can bend them down as well!) The other one is the modulation wheel, which usually lets you add *vibrato* to the sound. Some instruments have a joystick that replaces both wheels.

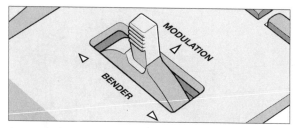

Bend the pitch up (to the right) or down (to the left), or move the stick forward to add modulation (Roland).

Synthesizers

Some keyboards have a synthesizer section. This allows you to modify the available sounds. You can make them shorter or longer, or you make them go from soft to loud, for example.

Sequencers

Most digital keyboard instruments allow you to record your own playing. The built-in recorder is usually referred to as a *sequencer*. It uses the same controls as a cassette recorder or MD recorder.

This basic sequencer allows you to record and play back four songs.

Disk drives and media cards

If an instrument has a floppy disk drive (FDD), you can use floppy disks to load new styles or songs, for example, and to store your performances and other data. A growing number of instruments use SmartMedia and other types of memory cards instead of floppy disks. Built-in hard disks and other media are used as well.

Pedals on pianos

Most acoustic pianos have two pedals. Depressing the one on the right makes the sound sustain after you release the keys. It is known as the *sustaining pedal* or *damper pedal*. The left pedal, which is usually called the *soft pedal*, is used to soften the volume and brightness of the sound. Digital pianos need to have at least a sustaining pedal.

13

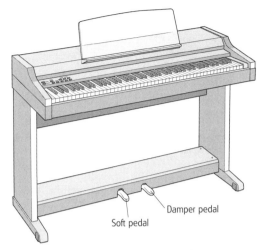

Digital piano with damper and soft pedals (Yamaha).

Pedals on keyboards

Most keyboards come without pedals. You can buy one or more of them as an option, though. A *volume pedal* or *expression pedal* is a popular choice, especially if you use a lot of organ and electric guitar sounds. There are also *pedal switches* that you can use to operate (start, stop, variation, etc.) the accompaniment, for example.

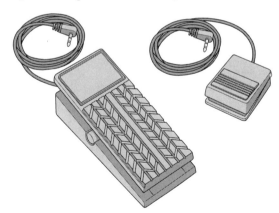

Continuous volume or expression pedal (left), and pedal switch.

Connections

The *connectors* for the instrument's pedals are usually located on the rear panel, together with one or more other connectors or *jacks*. *Line out jacks*, for example, can be

used to connect an external sound system; *line in jacks* allow you to have a CD player or another instrument play back through your main instrument's speakers. The headphone jack is usually located on the left side of the instrument, below the keyboard. Chapter 8 discusses the connections in more detail.

Rear panel of a keyboard, showing various inputs and outputs.

MIDI connections

One of the great features of keyboards and digital pianos is that you can hook them up to other instruments, or to your computer. This way, you can use one keyboard to control various instruments, or you can use your computer as a digital recording studio, or you can use the Internet as an interactive tutor – the possibilities are endless. The system that allows you to do so is called *MIDI*. This stands for *Musical Instrument Digital Interface*. Chapter 9 tells you more.

Power

Most digital keyboard instruments operate at 9 or 12 volts DC; an *adaptor* is required to convert the 110v or 230v current of the mains to this low voltage. Built-in adaptors need to be shielded very well to prevent hum. Because of this and various other reasons it's much cheaper to supply an external adaptor or offer one as an option, which is what most companies do. Some low-budget instruments can run on batteries too.

Other digital keyboard instruments

Many of the features mentioned here and elsewhere in this book can be found on a host of other digital keyboard instruments. They all have MIDI, for example, and sequencers are just as common. But there are also plenty of differences. Chapter 12 offers basic information on synthesizers, workstations, samplers, and related instruments.

3. LEARNING TO PLAY

Is it hard to learn to play a keyboard instrument? Yes and no, really. The layout of the keys itself is easy to understand. On the other hand, you need to get ten fingers to do exactly what you want them to, which can be pretty hard. The best answer is that it all depends on what you want to do.

If you've heard a tune somewhere, it's often easier to play it by ear on a keyboard instrument than on any other instrument. Why? Because one finger will do, and because all the notes are easy to find: higher notes to the right, lower ones to the left.

Easy

Keyboards are among the easiest instruments to get started on: The instrument's auto accompaniment and chord recognition features do a lot of the work for you. However, learning how to play it really well requires as much musicianship and practice as any other instrument. In terms of leaning to play, a digital piano is identical to an acoustic one.

Two parts

What makes both instruments different from most others is that you simultaneously play two parts: the melody with your right hand and the accompaniment with your left. On a piano, your left hand usually needs to do more than on a keyboard: Keyboards have chord recognition systems that allow you to play chords with one or two fingers. Pianos don't.

Reading music

Do you have to read music in order to play keyboard or piano? If you want to play classical music, the short answer is yes. If you're going to play anything else, then the answer is no, not necessarily – but being able to read music has a lot of advantages.

- It gives you access to **loads of books and magazines** with exercises, songs, and solos.
- It provides you with **better insight** into the way chords, songs, and compositions are structured.
- It enables you to **put down on paper** your own songs, ideas, and exercises, both for yourself and for other musicians.
- It makes you **more of a musician**.
- It **widens the range of gigs** you can play, so it broadens your career options.
- Learning to read music **isn't that hard at all**. *Tipbook Music on Paper – Basic Theory* (see page 134) teaches you the basics within a few chapters.
- What's more, some keyboard instruments have features to **help you learn** how to read music, understand chords, and so on.
- But when the time of the performance comes, just **forget about the notes**. You will play a lot better when you concentrate on the music instead of the notes. That's exactly why most keyboard players (including concert pianists!) don't use sheet music onstage.

Taking lessons

Many digital instruments have educational features that help you learn to play and practice, and you can find various interactive keyboard lessons on the Internet too. However, even the most advanced systems can't replace a 'real' teacher.

A good teacher

More than how to read music and play the right notes, a good teacher will teach you about a good technique, posture, dynamics, phrasing, and timing; how to interpret the music, what to study, or how to practice; how to use your talents and how to overcome your weak points… Just as important, your teacher can offer personal guidance and feedback.

Questions, questions

On your first visit to a teacher, don't just ask how much it costs. Here are some other questions.

- Is an **introductory lesson** included? This is a good way to find out how well you get on with the teacher and, for that matter, with the instrument.
- Will you be required to practice at least three hours a day, or can you also take lessons if you are just doing it **for the fun of it**?
- Do you need to buy a lot of books, or is **course material provided**?
- Is it possible to **record your lessons**, so you can go over the material again at home?
- Are you allowed to fully concentrate on **the style of music you want to play**, or will you be required – or encouraged – to learn other styles as well?
- Do you have to **practice scales** for two years, or will you be allowed to play songs as soon as possible?
- Is advice on **purchasing instruments** and other equipment included?

Locating a teacher

Looking for a private teacher? Music stores may have teachers on staff, or they can refer you to one. You can also consult the Internet (see pages 133–134), your local Musicians' Union, or the band director at a high school in your vicinity. And you can check the classified ads in newspapers, in music magazines, or on supermarket bulletin boards, or consult a copy of the *Yellow Pages*. Professional private teachers will usually charge between twenty and fifty dollars per hour. Some make house calls, for which you'll pay extra.

Music schools

You also may want to check whether there is a keyboard school, a teacher collective, or a music school in your vicinity. These organizations may offer extras such as ensemble playing, master classes, and clinics, in a wide variety of styles and at various levels.

Group or individual tuition

You can take individual lessons, but you can also go for group tuition if that's an option in your area. Personal

tuition is more expensive, but it can be tailored exactly to your needs.

PRACTICE

One of the great advantages of playing an electronic instrument is that you can practice without bothering your neighbors or housemates. Just pop on some headphones or turn the volume down, and you can practice day and night.

Piano?

If you want to learn to play the piano, it's best to practice on a digital or an acoustic piano. A piano teacher may not accept you as a student if you have a keyboard instead: They are quite different instruments, as explained on pages 6–9.

Digital vs. acoustic

Even though digital pianos are getting to sound and feel more like acoustic ones, they're still not the same. You will have to make adjustments if you practice on one and have your lessons on the other.

Keyboards

Keyboard teachers will often recommend that you have at least a 61-note instrument.

Half an hour

How much practice you need depends on your talent and on where you want to end. Many top players spent years practicing for four hours a day or even longer. The more you practice, the faster you'll learn. Most people make noticeable progress when practicing for half an hour a day, though.

Three times ten

If you find it hard to practice half an hour at a time, try dividing it up into two quarter-hour sessions, or three of ten minutes each.

Practicing tools

Many digital keyboard instruments have one or more

features that make practicing easier. For one thing, you can use the onboard sequencer to record the right-hand part of the music. Then play that back and practice the left hand along with the recording, at a tempo you can handle. Many instruments even offer a number of pre-recorded songs: You can have the instrument play one hand while you play the other. There's more about these and other options on pages 70–71.

Books, videos, DVDs, CDs...

Besides a teacher, your instrument, and the Internet, there are even more sources that can help you improve as a player.

- **Songbooks** contain transcriptions of songs that you can play.
- You can also get **full accompaniments** for the songs you want to learn to play, either on floppy disk or on the Internet.
- You can play along with **your favorite CDs**. This is even easier if your instrument has a special input for that purpose (see page 95).
- **Instructional videos and DVDs**, often created and presented by well-known musicians, can be very inspiring.
- **Keyboard magazines and websites** (see pages 133–134) often publish useful playing tips, as well as transcriptions and exercises.

Play a lot

Finally, one of the best ways to learn to play is seeing other musicians at work. Living legends or local amateurs – every concert or gig can be a learning experience. And the very best way to learn to play? Play a lot!

4. BUYING AN INSTRUMENT

You can get a keyboard for less than a hundred dollars, but that might not be the best choice if you're serious about making music. So how much should you spend, and what will that get you? Here are some basic considerations and useful pre-shopping tips.

Talking about prices for electronic musical instruments can be risky. One example: When this book came out, a keyboard with a built-in floppy disk drive was available for some three hundred dollars. Three or four years before, you'd easily pay three times as much.

Three hundred and up

A decent entry-level keyboard that offers sufficient sound quality and the necessary features to keep you happy for a few years will usually cost from three hundred dollars upwards. Most cheaper keyboards can be used to get acquainted with music, to help you with ear training, or just to fool around with, but they're not designed to suit the needs of aspiring musicians.

Lots of everything

For those three hundred odd dollars you have a choice of keyboards that look fairly spectacular, with an impressive amount of controls, hundreds of sounds, and a hundred different styles or more. So is there any sense in spending more?

Three thousand and up

Yes, there is, as there's usually more than meets the eye.

First of all, more expensive instruments usually sound better (see Chapter 6). They offer a greater range of sounds (Chapter 5) and accompaniments (Chapter 7). They feature more powerful sequencers (Chapter 5), more inputs and outputs (Chapters 8 and 9), and they're often easier to work with due to a higher quality user interface (Chapter 5, again). A top-of-the-range keyboard may set you back three thousand dollars or more – without the optional pedals, hard disks, and other accessories.

Digital pianos
Digital pianos, on average, are more expensive than keyboards. They usually have more keys (88) and a more complicated key mechanism, higher quality samples, and a better and more powerful sound system to realistically reproduce piano sounds, and some even have a wooden cabinet.

Prices
You can get a portable digital piano with an 88-note hammer-action keyboard for a thousand dollars or less. Instruments of similar quality sporting a full cabinet may start around that price, but most models cost considerably more. Digital ensemble pianos (hammer action keys, auto accompaniment, numerous sounds) usually start upwards of two thousand dollars. Prices of digital grand pianos range from five to fifteen thousand dollars and more.

Acoustic or digital?
Though digital pianos are getting closer and closer, they're still not identical to acoustic instruments. One major difference is that the sound of a digital piano is goes through two or more loudspeakers, while an acoustic piano has a huge wooden soundboard. This is just one of the reasons why many pianists – especially the ones who play classical music – will always prefer an acoustic instrument.*

Acoustic
Acoustic pianos are generally more expensive than their digital counterparts. They need to be tuned at least twice a year, they need maintenance, and changes in humidity

---

* See Tipbook Piano (page 134).

and temperature can affect their performance. They're also difficult (read: expensive) to move. Most acoustic pianos are higher and deeper than digital models, though the amount of floor space they need isn't that much bigger. Apart from subjective differences in sound and feel, acoustic pianos have the advantage that they can last a lifetime, and they retain most of their value if they're well maintained. Digital pianos don't.

Acoustic and digital

You can find the strengths of both acoustic and digital pianos in a *hybrid piano*: an acoustic instrument with an onboard sound module (see page 120).

SHOPPING

If you have decided to get yourself a keyboard or a digital piano, go visit friends and neighbors who own one. Ask if you can play their instrument, and find out what they think of their equipment. Experienced users can also shed light on the usefulness – or uselessness – of certain features.

Wait

Don't just buy from the first shop that happens to stock what you want, unless you fall head over heels in love with a certain instrument – and even then it may be a good idea to wait. Spend some time shopping around. Listen to a variety of instruments, and listen to a variety of sales people; they have their own 'sound' as well.

Make notes

It's hard to keep track of every detail of every instrument. So why not take notes when you're in the shop? Or do it the other way around: Make a list of everything you want your instrument to do (reading this book will help you compile this list), and ask the sales staff which models fit the bill.

A little more

Once you have your eye on an instrument, take one more look at the next model on the price list. Some fifty or a hundred dollars more may buy you useful features such as editable effects, pitch bend, or modulation.

Demo

Avoid sales staff who restrict their input to hitting the demo button. Also remember that it will take quite some time to learn to play the instrument as well as the one who performed the demo.

A good store

Buying musical instruments is mostly a matter of comparing their sounds. You can do so only if you can play a few different instruments in the same room, on the same day. A good store offers sufficient stock and plenty of time to play-test instruments, as well as personal advice.

Online and mail-order

Buying online or by mail-order makes it impossible to compare sounds, styles, the feel of the keys, the user interface… However, online and mail-order companies usually offer a return service for most or all of their products: If you're not happy with your purchase, you can send it back within a certain period of time. Of course the instrument should be in new condition when you do.

Eighty percent

As technology progresses, keyboards in particular tend to depreciate rapidly. They can lose up to eighty percent of their value within two or three years. The sunny side? Electronic instruments are frequently sold at bargain prices to make room for the latest models.

USED INSTRUMENTS

Pre-owned digital instruments are available at very modest prices. Here are a few more things to think about.

The very latest

Older instruments won't have all the latest music styles, simply because these styles didn't exist at the time the keyboard was built. This is no problem if the instrument can be updated (see pages 67–68 and 85).

Privately or in a store?

Purchasing a used instrument from a private party may be cheaper than buying the same one from a store. One of the

advantages of buying used instruments in a store, though, is that you can go back if you have questions: Good advice and service are often invaluable where musical instruments are concerned. Also, some music stores may offer you a limited warranty on your purchase. Another difference is that a good dealer won't usually ask an outrageous price, but a private seller might – because he doesn't know any better, or because he thinks that you don't.

Where?

The best place to look for used instruments is in the classified ads section of music magazines and newspapers, on the Internet, and on bulletin boards in stores and supermarkets. Alternatively, you could submit or post an ad yourself.

ANYTHING ELSE?

It's always a good idea to bring along an experienced keyboard player, maybe your teacher, when you go out shopping – particularly when buying a pre-owned instrument. Two see and hear more than one, even if you have learned this book by heart.

Catalogs, magazines, and the Internet

Catalogs, brochures, and the Internet can provide you with detailed information outlining the differences and similarities between a wide variety of models and brands. Various magazines and websites offer reviews of the latest gear and plenty of additional information (see pages 133–134).

Fairs and conventions

Visit music trade fairs, demo sessions, clinics, and music conventions if and when you can. Besides finding a considerable number of instruments to try out and compare, you will also meet plenty of product specialists and many fellow musicians, many of whom can be good sources of information and inspiration.

5. A GOOD INSTRUMENT

They may all look pretty much the same, but they're not. Both keyboards and digital pianos can differ widely in quality and capabilities. This chapter deals with most of the features that you can more or less judge without playing a single note.

The information in this and the following chapters is meant to help you select an instrument, and to help you understand the instrument you have. Chapter 6 deals with sound, while auto accompaniment systems are covered in Chapter 7. Chapter 8 explains the various types of connections you may come across, and Chapter 9 is about MIDI.

KEYBOARDS AND KEYS

The quality of the keyboard is a major factor in how much you enjoy playing an instrument and how easy it is to control the sound.

Piano keys

Most digital pianos have 88 keys, just like most acoustic pianos. Models with 76 keys are usually made to offer a less expensive alternative to the consumer, to have an instrument that's easier to carry around, or to help save space. Some pianos are available with either 88 or 76 keys; the latter can cost up to some 30 percent less.

Classical music or jazz

Though a large part of the repertoire can be played on those 76 keys, it is generally recommended to get an 88-

note piano if you want to play classical music or jazz. In other styles of music, you will rarely miss those seven low and five high notes.

C1 to C8

All 88-note instruments have eight C keys. The lowest one, on the far left, is called C1; the highest is C8. Each note in between has a corresponding name, *e.g.*, the A above C4 is A4.

Five octaves

Most serious keyboards are five-octave instruments, sporting 61 keys. Some have 76, and a few are available with either 61 or 76 keys. As you can make the entire instrument sound one or more octaves higher or lower, a 61-note keyboard will allow you to play the very highest and the very lowest notes (transposing; see page 53). Having more keys at hand, however, gives you access to a larger range without having to adjust the octaves.

Exception

Instruments with an identical number of keys usually cover the same range (see illustration), except for those with 73 keys: Some of these go from E1 to E7, others from F1 to F7, or from C1 to C7.

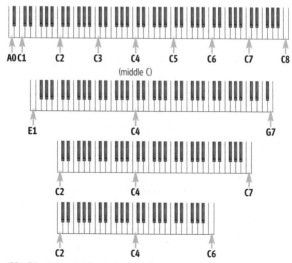

88-, 76-, 61-, and 49-note keyboards.

Key shape

White keys come in various shapes. Most keyboard and synthesizers have *overhanging* or *synth-type* keys. Digital pianos usually have *piano-style* keys, also known as *box-type* keys.

Waterfall

A third type of key, the *square-front* or *waterfall* key, can be found on Hammond organs (see page 117) and some instruments that emulate that type of sound. Waterfall keys look like piano-style keys without the small protruding lip at the front. They're usually combined with black keys with rounded off fronts. This design is best for playing glissandos, smearing your hand across the keys from left too right, or vice versa. Glisses are harder to do on synth-type keys, which can easily catch your skin.

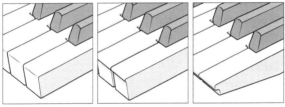

Square-front or waterfall keys (l), piano-style or box-type keys, and synth-style or overhanging keys (r).

Hammer action

On acoustic pianos, the keys trigger felt-tipped hammers to hit the strings. The moving hammers and the weight of the construction give the instrument its characteristic playing action. To emulate this type of action, good digital pianos have a key mechanism that includes a small hammer whose only purpose is to provide the desired 'acoustic' feel. This is commonly known as a (*weighted*) *hammer action*, *hammered action*, or *piano-action* keyboard.

Synth-action

Keyboards, synthesizers, and organs have *synth-action* or *non-weighted* keys. Contrary to piano-action keys, they use springs to return to their original position.

The difference

Hammer-action keyboards are heavier to play and require

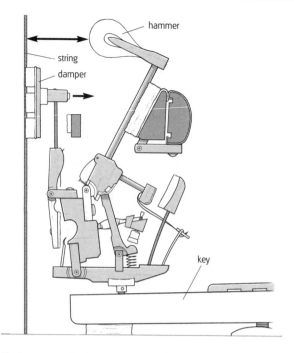

The hammer mechanism in an acoustic piano. The downward
motion of the key simultaneously makes the hammer hit the string
and releases the damper. On releasing the key, the damper falls
back into place, muting the string.

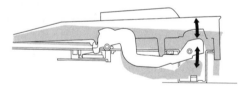

Hammer action. The hammer, just beneath the key, helps to mimic the
action of an acoustic piano.

more practice and strength, but they provide more control
over the tone and allow for expressive playing, just as
acoustic pianos do. If you're a pianist, a synth-action
keyboard will feel soggy or toy-like; if you're used to a
synth-action keyboard, a piano-action will feel heavy and
stiff – but you can get used to playing both.

Wooden keys and more

To mimic the feel of an acoustic piano as well as possible,
digital pianos often have balanced wooden keys, which

provide an even feel all along the keyboard. Some also emulate the feel of other parts of the acoustic piano mechanism, such as the *let-off* or *escapement*. And as the lower notes of the acoustic instrument use heavier hammers and dampers than the higher ones, a growing number of digital instruments also emulate that effect, which is known as *scaled hammer effect* or *graded hammer action*.

Semi-weighted keys

A *semi-weighted* keyboard has keys that feel heavier than those of a synth-action keyboard, but they don't imitate acoustic piano keys. If you don't like the 'floppy' or heavy feel of a hammer-action keyboard or the light keys of a synth-type keyboard, this might be what you're looking for.

Confusing

You may find the term 'weighted keyboard' to be used for what's described above as a semi-weighted keyboard, while others use it to indicate a hammer-action keyboard.

The feel

When you compare instruments, you'll find that the key action may feel very different from one keyboard to another, or from one piano to another: light or heavy, fast or sluggish, precise or lumpy…. What's best has as much to do with quality as with your preferences or your style of playing. Always turn on the instrument before checking the feel of the keys: They won't feel good (and they're all too noisy) when there's no sound. Also check the keys for an even response all along the keyboard.

Touch sensitivity

Almost every digital keyboard instrument is *touch sensitive*: The harder you hit the keys, the louder the sound will be. When you play harder, you actually move the keys down faster. It is this velocity (speed) which is measured and translated into a louder or a softer sound. This is why this feature is also referred to as *velocity sensitivity*.

Not just louder

As you hit an acoustic piano key harder, the sound not only becomes louder, but a bit brighter too. Guitars, violins, and most other instruments respond in a similar way.

High-quality keyboard instruments are capable of reproducing those subtle changes (see page 75).

Keyboard touch response

On many pianos you can set the keyboard touch response, adapting the degree of sensitivity to your playing style. Set to *light* or *soft* you don't need a pianist's technique to produce loud notes. The *hard* or *heavy* setting will give you the widest dynamic range – from a whisper to a roar. The number of settings or *velocity curves* varies from three to more than a hundred. On some, you can also design and store your personal touch curve. This won't alter the action: It just changes the way the keys respond to your playing.

Harpsichords and organs

A number of acoustic keyboard instruments, such as harpsichords and organs, are not touch sensitive. If you want to truly reproduce such instruments, you need to be able to turn off the touch sensitivity. In some cases this happens automatically when you select one of these sounds. If so, you need a volume pedal (see page 37) to be able to vary the loudness of your organ sounds.

Aftertouch

Some instruments offer a second stage of touch sensitivity that kicks in once the key has been depressed. This is known as *aftertouch*: By pushing the key down a little further, you add a little extra color or volume to the sound, or another layer, or vibrato (modulation), or pitch bend, for example. The effect may depend on the instrument, on the chosen sound (some instruments select an effect that works best for the sound you play), or on your settings.

Channel or polyphonic

A few instruments have *polyphonic aftertouch*, meaning that only the pressed note is affected. This requires one pressure sensitive sensor per key. *Channel aftertouch* has one sensor for the entire keyboard, so all currently sounding notes will be affected.

Release velocity

An instrument with *release velocity* is also sensitive to how quickly you let the keys go. This allows you to fade out

strings gently as you bring up the keys, rather than chopping them off, for example.

Multipads

On many keyboards, sounds can also be triggered by a series of *multipads*. Hitting these pads often activates drum, percussion, or effect sounds, but it can also trigger fill-ins or backing phrases (a horn section or a guitar riff to spice up the accompaniment, for example), or even pre-arranged solos. Not all multipads or *touch pads* are touch sensitive.

Multipads.

Assignable pads

On a growing number of instruments you can assign or *map* sounds, effects, or phrases to the pads. It may also be possible to use the pads to access other functions, such as selecting a pre-programmed style or sound, or turn on an effect for a solo.

CONTROLLERS

Every digital keyboard instrument has a variety of controllers, ranging from knobs and sliders to wheels and joysticks.

Fixed or assignable

The volume control is usually a *fixed function control*: You can't assign it to do anything else than adjusting the volume. Many controllers on keyboards perform more than one function. If you can assign a variety of functions to a controller yourself, you're dealing with an *assignable controller*.

Faders

A fader is a sliding controller. Quite often, one fader is used to perform various functions, ranging from control-

ling volume to setting effects, tempo, or a time signature (*e.g.*, $\frac{4}{4}$, $\frac{6}{8}$).

Rotary controllers

These and many other functions can also be controlled by *rotary controllers* or *endless controllers* – controllers that can be rotated endlessly, rather than from 1 to 10. If a value has been set to 48, for example, and you turn the relevant controller up, it will start at 48 and increase the value from there.

Soft keys

If you have a cell phone, you know what *soft keys* are: They're the keys on the perimeter of a display. Their functions change according to the information being shown on the display. On keyboards, they can be used for a huge number of different things, from selecting sounds to setting effects. An illustration is shown on page 45.

Touch screen

On an instrument with a *touch screen* or *touch panel* display you make selections by touching 'buttons' that are displayed on the screen.

Pitch bend and vibrato   Tipcode KEYS-006

Two of the most widely used effects are pitch bend and vibrato or modulation. You'll find them on most serious keyboards and some pianos. Many instruments have a wheel controller for each function. The wheel that controls pitch bend is usually self-centering: It jumps back as soon as you let go of it, returning to normal pitch. The wheel that controls modulation usually has to be returned to its

Joystick; pitch-bend and modulation wheels.

'neutral' position by hand. If there's a joystick that controls both pitch bend (moving it sideways) and modulation (moving it away from you), it's commonly self-centering for both effects.

Pitch bend

Pitch bend is essential if you want to play realistic guitar or wind instrument parts, for example. The degree of pitch bend is often programmable. Though typically set to bend up or down one whole note, it may be able to go up and down as much as an octave or more.

Modulation

'Modulation,' for keyboard players, has grown to mean vibrato (a rapid pitch variation). Turning the modulation wheel up or moving the joystick away from you will increase the depth of the effect. Vibrato is essential to playing realistic string and wind instrument sounds.

Other effects

Some keyboards allow you to assign other effects or functions to the modulation wheel, ranging from volume control to filters (see page 66), wah-wah effects, tremolo, and more.

Ribbon controllers

On some instruments, you control pitch bend, modulation, and other effects with a *ribbon controller* or *touch controller*. You just slide your finger over the ribbon to bend the pitch up or to increase the vibrato depth, for example.

Infrared light

Many buildings have doors that automatically open as you approach. Some keyboards have a similar feature: By moving your hand through an invisible field of infrared light, you can control a variety of effects and functions, bend pitch, start or stop parts or all of the accompaniment, or slow down the tempo of the song...

Real-time controllers

Pitch-bend and modulation wheels, ribbons, and beams are perfect examples of *real-time controllers*: You can use them to change settings while you play in 'real time,' making

for much more expressive and natural performances. Some instruments feature *breath control*. This allows you to control wind instrument sounds by breath pressure, varying the loudness by blowing harder or softer.

Drawbars

Tipcode KEYS-007

Drawbars are best known from the Hammond tone wheel organs, which are portrayed on page 117. When using organ sounds, these sliders add higher and lower *overtones* or *harmonics* to the notes you're playing. This imitates the effect of using *organ flutes* of various lengths (see page 115), allowing you to determine the exact timbre of your organ sound. If you use the 16' drawbar, it is as if you add the sound of a 16-foot organ flute to the note you play. This drawbar produces a note that sounds one octave below the pitch you are playing.

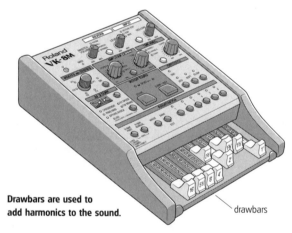

**Drawbars are used to
add harmonics to the sound.**

drawbars

High and low

The 8' drawbar represents the actual note you are playing: If you close it, you don't hear that pitch anymore. The 4' drawbar adds the pitch of the first overtone or harmonic of the note you play. This overtone sounds an octave higher. Opening the 2 ⅔' drawbar adds the second overtone, a fifth above the first one.

Shorter but bassier

Though the 5 ⅓' drawbar adds a higher frequency to the note you play (after all, it is 'shorter' than 8'), it actually tends to make for a fuller, bassier sound.

Table

The table below shows what the drawbars do when you play the note C4 (Middle C). Adding harmonics makes for a broader, richer sound, as you can easily hear.

Drawbar	Overtones	Example
16'	Subharmonic	C3
5 1/3'	Fifth above fundamental	G4
8'	Fundamental	C4
4'	First overtone	C5
2 2/3'	Second overtone	G5
1 3/5'	Fourth overtone	E6
1 1/3'	Fifth overtone	G6
1'	Seventh overtone	C7

The drawbars and the harmonics they add to the tone. The last row shows the pitches that they add when you play Middle C (C4).

Virtual drawbars

Many keyboards have *virtual drawbars*: Their settings, usually adjustable by soft keys, are shown on-screen. Other designs use LEDs to show the settings for each drawbar, and up/down buttons to control them.

Controllers: check

Checking out the controllers themselves can give you an impression of the overall quality of the instrument. Feel how they work and check knobs, switches, and wheels for play: They should only move in the intended direction. Some instruments have countersunk controls, which are less likely to snap off when you carry the instrument around or put it in a gig bag.

PEDALS

Pedals can be used to perform a host of different functions.

Pedals for pianos

In an acoustic piano, the sustaining pedal or damper pedal is used to move the dampers from and to the strings. The pedal mechanism lets you control how fast this happens, and you can vary the distance between dampers and strings. On good digital pianos you can perform these *half pedal* and other pedal techniques, which require a *continuous*

pedal. A single, continuous piano-style pedal usually costs between twenty-five and fifty dollars.

Switch

Cheaper instruments sometimes use a footswitch that allows for dampers on or off only. Note that there are continuous pedals that look like the switch pictured below.

A continuous piano-style pedal and a footswitch.

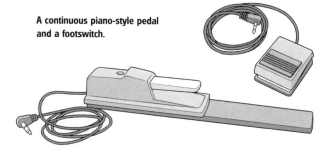

On the left

On acoustic pianos, the left pedal (piano pedal or *soft pedal*) reduces the volume and slightly changes the tone. Digital pianos emulate this electronically. Serious pianists need this pedal, which is often combined with a damper pedal in one unit.

In the middle

Many upmarket digital pianos have a third, middle pedal, known as the *sostenuto pedal.* Play a chord, then depress the pedal; the chord will be sustained, while any further notes you play won't. This pedal is required for a limited number of compositions only. A piano with three pedals is shown on page 39.

Volume or expression pedals

The organ is not a touch sensitive instrument. Instead, you use a *volume pedal* or *expression pedal* to control the volume. Keyboards become a lot more expressive when you add such a pedal – when you use organ sounds, but also guitars and wind instruments can be made to sound much more convincing. Controlling the volume with a pedal has a different effect than using the keyboard's touch sensitivity. Expression pedals can be used for other functions too (wah-wah, modulation, and so on). Prices

range from less than thirty to more than a hundred fifty dollars.

Multiswitch

Also available are (*MIDI*) *foot controllers* or *multiswitches* with as many as ten or more assignable switches that allow hands-free operation of a variety of tasks (start, stop, next sound or style, fill, ending…). Some also include a continuous pedal. Depending on the quality and the number of switches or pedals and what they can do, such units usually cost anywhere from one to four hundred dollars.

Connections

Basic keyboards may have room for a single pedal only (usually allowing for a continuous damper or expression pedal, or an assignable switch); more advanced models offer more connections. An assignable pedal input allows you to choose what you want the pedal to do: change volume level, control 'dampers,' select the next sound or style, and so on. Note that some instruments require specific multiswitches or pedals.

Bass pedals

Keyboards may have an input jack for a *bass pedal keyboard* with up to some thirty oversized keys, on which you can play bass parts with your feet – just like a real organ player. Some of these pedals can also be used to play harmonies, drums, percussion sounds, or effects, or to control MIDI functions (see Chapter 9). Prices vary from a couple of hundred to two thousand dollars and more.

Rugged and non-slip

If you want to use a pedal onstage, go for one that's rugged enough to withstand some abuse. It should have a non-slip bottom too.

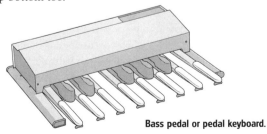

Bass pedal or pedal keyboard.

THE HOUSING

If you plan to play an instrument in your living room, looks will play a role in your selection. For instruments that are going to be used onstage, solidity and weight will be more relevant.

Stage pianos and keyboards

Higher quality stage pianos often have a rugged metal chassis, which makes the instrument both road-tough and heavy. Professional stage pianos easily weigh fifty pounds or more. Keyboards are considerably lighter: This makes them easier to handle but they're also quite vulnerable. If you take any keyboard instrument on the road, make sure to pack it in a good bag or case (see pages 111–112).

Matching stand

Some portable instruments come with an optional matching stand. A few companies make matching stands with built-in piano-style pedals.

Music rest

Onboard music rests come in a lot of different guises, varying from plasticized wire frames that can be clipped onto the instrument to heavily sculptured designs. They're not always included.

Spinets, consoles, and grands

Most digital pianos look more or less like small upright acoustic *spinet pianos* (up to some forty inches high) or

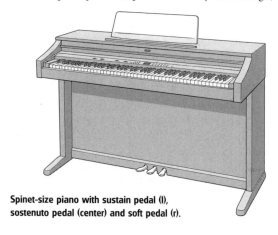

**Spinet-size piano with sustain pedal (l),
sostenuto pedal (center) and soft pedal (r).**

slightly larger *console* or *studio* pianos (up to about forty-five inches). Digital grand pianos are generally smaller than acoustic models. Their sizes range from around 27.5" (68cm) to 5'9" (175 cm).

Single panel or sound box
Most pianos have a single panel under the keyboard, as shown on page 39. Other models have a large sound box instead, making them look more like an acoustic instrument.

Real wood vs. wood-grain
Real wood cabinets are considerably more expensive than cabinets made of another material (*e.g.*, MDF) that has been covered with a *wood-grain* or *simulated wood* finish. Some companies claim that a wood construction enhances the sound, making it warmer and more natural.

The more you pay
The more you pay, the more your digital piano will usually look like an acoustic instrument, with brass plated pedals and caster wheels, a sculptured music rack, a matching bench, and so on. Modern designs are also available, with stainless steel bodies, metal finishes, and wooden side panels... Bigger instruments often sound better because they house bigger and better speakers, and appropriate amplification.

Finishes
Both wood and wood-grain instruments come in a wide variety of finishes, from rosewood and gloss mahogany to cherry, polished ebony, and Mediterranean oak satin.

Weight
Full cabinet digital pianos are easier to handle and to move than their acoustic cousins, yet they can be quite heavy, up to some three hundred pounds (135 kilos). Digital grand pianos can be even heavier.

Benches
Some digital pianos come with a matching bench or offer one as an option. Height adjustable benches are available for as little as fifty dollars. Spending more may get you more comfortable cushioning, infinite height adjustment,

a sheet music compartment below the seat, and legs with leveling adjusters that keep the bench from wobbling on uneven floors.

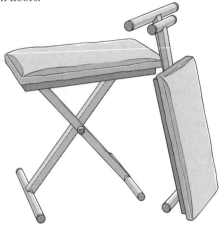

Basic height-adjustable, and collapsible bench.

DISPLAYS

The display keeps you informed about what you (and your instrument) are doing. There are two basic display types: numeric and LCD.

Numeric

A *numeric display* is usually limited to showing a few numbers or letters, presenting information in an abbreviated form. For example, T112 would mean that the tempo (T) is set at 112 *beats per minute* (*bpm*), or SO34 would indicate that you're using sound (SO) number 34. You'll find this type of display on the least expensive keyboards, but

A numeric display.

also on digital pianos that have a limited number of features and therefore don't require complex displays. In fact, some pianos don't have a display at all.

Liquid crystals

Most instruments have a *graphic display*, similar to the one of a cell phone, known as *LCD* (*Liquid Crystal Display*). On keyboards and ensemble pianos, the display shows a host of information, ranging from the selected sounds, tempo, and style, to the chords and the keys you're playing, volume and effect settings, and so on. A large display can provide simultaneous access to a lot of information, it has room for larger, easier-to-read type and graphic icons, and it's less likely to use puzzling abbreviations such as vRomtcTp (a vibrating trumpet sound…).

A display showing the accompaniment, the tempo, the effects and sounds that are being used, and more.

Pixels

The number of pixels, often specified in seductive phrases like 'large 320x240 display,' doesn't tell you anything about the physical size of the display. If you have two equally sized displays, the one with the higher pixel count has a higher resolution, meaning that it produces a more defined image.

Color

On full-color displays, the colors can be used to enhance the presentation and organization of the information. For example, some screens change color to indicate which style, song, record, or other mode you are in.

Adjustable angle

The visibility of the display can be improved if its angle is

adjustable – which rarely is the case. Some displays lock flat for easier transportation.

Visibility

A *contrast control* helps to improve the readability of the display under various lighting conditions. If it gets really dark, you will need a *backlit display*, which is illuminated from behind. Some instruments have illuminated buttons as well. If the display lights up only if you're touching the controls of the instrument (similar to cell phones), it doesn't distract you when you're playing. Very few instruments have sockets that allow you to connect a gooseneck lamp.

Sheet music and lyrics

Some instruments can also display sheet music and lyrics, which advance as you play. Instruments that feature a karaoke system often allow you to connect a TV or another type of monitor so others can sing along (i.e., *multimedia keyboards*). The required video interface may be included or optional. Others also offer the possibility to display a slide show of your digital images.

... sheet music and lyrics advance as you play...

USER-FRIENDLINESS

The way information is organized on the display is a major factor in how user-friendly an instrument is, but there's more.

High button count

A high button count may look intimidating, but it has its advantages: If the most common features have dedicated

buttons, knobs, or faders, they're easier to access than having a limited number of buttons that you need to press seven times before you reach the option that you want.

Without the manual

Menus and submenus should be well-organized. Ideally, you should be able to make the instrument do everything you want to do without using the manual – but very few instruments are that user-friendly. Advanced instruments often provide a *help* function.

User-friendly?

What else makes an instrument more user-friendly? A well-organized layout of the controls. A number of buttons that you can program to memorize the sounds and styles you use most. A *help* tool, triggered perhaps by pressing the relevant button for longer than two seconds. An intuitive way to go from one screen to the other (and back!). Vocal cues that announce functions. A panic or exit button that allows you to go back to the previous menu or the instrument's home page. A display that offers the relevant information as soon as you activate a certain function. An instrument that uses other languages too (some speak as many as six) – and so on…

SELECTING SOUNDS AND STYLES

There are many different systems for selecting sounds and accompaniments on keyboards. Pianos are simpler, so that's where this section starts.

Two at a time

Pianos with a limited number of sounds usually have a dedicated button for each available sound. Voices can often be layered by simply pushing two buttons at a time.

Groupings

On keyboards and (ensemble) pianos that feature lots of sounds, the sounds are usually grouped into *banks*, *sound families*, or *sound categories*. Each group contains a number of related sounds – pianos in group one, chromatic percussion (vibraphone, glockenspiel, etc.) in group two, organs in group three, guitars in group four, and so on.

Accompaniments are usually grouped by style – pop, Latin, jazz, dance, and so on, with each group containing a variety of patterns.

Calling up sounds

Lower-budget instruments often list numbered sounds and styles on the front panel. You choose a style or sound by punching in the corresponding number on a numeric keypad, or by using button combinations. If the baritone saxophone is sound number 14 in group B, you push button B first, followed by buttons 1 and 4.

On display

If an instrument has more sounds and styles than can be printed on the front panel, you usually make your selec-

Selecting sounds and accompaniments using a numeric keypad.

Soft keys allow you to find the desired guitar sound (GEM).

tions from the display, by using soft keys or virtual controls on a touch screen, for example.

Data entry wheel

Many instruments use a *data entry wheel* to scroll sounds or styles. Data entry wheels, also known as *jog wheels* or *alpha dials*, are commonly used to select tempo, assign sounds to multipads, and perform other jobs too.

Data entry wheel.

Enter button

If you use a data entry wheel to scroll sounds or styles, you'll usually have to press an *enter* button to confirm your choice.

Variations

Instruments often offer one or more variations on their sounds. Variations on a saxophone voice, for example, might include that same saxophone with a vibrato, or with a chorus. Some variations can be very subtle: a grand piano sample, for instance, with varying degrees to which the lid is opened and the display showing the corresponding lid angle. In other cases, variations would be voices of related instruments: an upright bass, an electric bass guitar, and a fretless bass guitar, for example.

Search engine

If you have hundreds of sounds or styles to choose from, a *search engine* makes life much easier. Finding styles can

Wide open, completely closed, or anything in between.

be facilitated when you can group them in various ways (*e.g.*, category, era, alphabetical…). On some instruments, you can find songs by playing the first few notes of the melody. These and many other features are getting more and more common.

Demo per sound

A few instruments offer demos that illustrate the specific characteristics of each voice individually. This can be of great help when selecting sounds, or getting to know each voice and its possibilities.

Direct piano

The grand piano voice is the single most popular sound, both on digital pianos and on keyboards. That explains why quite a lot of keyboards have a 'direct piano' or 'piano setting' button that activates the instrument's very best piano sound and puts the keyboard in the full mode, so it can be played like a 'real' piano.

One touch

Keyboards often call up sounds that match the chosen styles automatically: a tenor saxophone for a jazzy ballad, a trumpet for salsa… Calling up that sound is a matter of pressing a button labeled *one touch* or *single touch*, for example. Appropriate effects and layers may be chosen automatically as well. Some instruments even provide you with a choice of two, three, or more matching instruments.

One key, various sounds   Tipcode KEYS-008

With certain voices, there may be different samples under each key – for example, a jazz scat voice that triggers different scat sounds depending on how hard you hit the keys: '*du*,' '*dap*,' '*daooooow*'…

SPLITS

When you use the split function, the two resulting keyboard sections are often called *upper* and *lower*. These names stem from the upper and lower keyboard or manual of so-called *dual manual organs* (see pages 115 and 117). On these instruments, each manual or keyboard has its own (drawbar) settings.

Split point

On most instruments, you can set the split point yourself. This is known as a *floating* or *programmable split*. If you set it at C3, this will be the lowest note for the upper (right hand) section. Multiple splits are less common, but there are keyboards than you can divide into a number of zones, each with its own sound. These zones can then be assigned their own pitch as well (transposing, see page 53). This means that you can, for example, alternate between a sax and a trumpet, playing them at identical pitches in different areas of the keyboard.

Balance

For a musical performance, it is important that you can adjust the volume level for each voice independently.

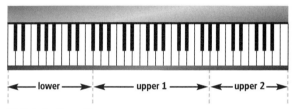

←— lower —→ ←— upper 1 —→ ←— upper 2 —→

Multiple floating splits

Chord recognition

If you're using the chord recognition feature of a keyboard (*e.g.*, *arranger mode*), you can usually determine where the split between the chord recognition area and the upper section occurs.

LAYERS

With most instruments you can layer two sounds, and a few allow you to stack more sounds on top of that. The various voices of a layered sound in the upper part of the keyboard are usually labeled *upper 1* or *upper orchestra 1*, *upper 2*, and so on. The lower half of the keyboard may have a layering option as well.

Flexibility

The more layers you have available, the more flexible you can be in creating your own sounds. For instance, you could use four layers to make up your own horn section,

either a traditional one, with a trumpet, an alto sax, and two tenor saxes, or an alternative quartet of a soprano sax, a trombone, and two tubas. Or you can use multiple layers to create a broad, fat-sounding string section by blending several string sounds at slightly different pitches.

Separate buttons

Some instruments have a separate button for each sound you can select in a performance. This allows you to play all those sounds simultaneously by just pressing the corresponding buttons, or to switch from one voice to the other, so you can play call and response choruses by yourself: four bars sax solo, four bars guitar, four bars piano, four bars guitar – and so on.

Transpose

If you can transpose the sounds in a layer independently, you can create nice textures: Play a piano solo and let a string section play along a fifth higher, for example, or use two keyboard sounds for a fuller effect.

Combinations

Layers and splits can often be used in a wide variety of combinations. One example is to use the lower part of the keyboard for one sound, the upper part for another, and add strings to both.

VOLUME AND BALANCE

Layers, splits, and accompaniments bring a great number of volume levels into play. Ideally, the volume of each part or section should be independently controllable, just as it would be in a recording studio. The more sophisticated the instrument, the more independent volume controls will generally be available.

For a musical performance, it helps if you're able to adjust the balances between the various sounds in a layer, between the lower and upper sections of a split keyboard, and between the accompaniment and the melody. A few instruments have *style touch sensitivity*, allowing you to control the volume of the accompaniment in real time, simply by how hard you play the chords in the lower section of the keyboard.

Accompaniment balance

You may also be able to adjust the balance of the various *tracks* of the accompaniment. A typical arrangement might have four volume controls marked *bass*, *drums*, *acc1*, and *acc2*. The sounds used for the parts labeled *acc1* and *acc2* can vary: a piano and a brass section in one style, or a funky guitar and strings in another, and so on.

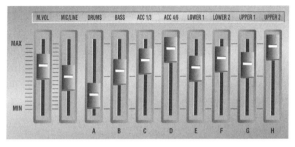

Separate controls for master volume, microphone level, drums, bass, accompaniments 1 to 3, and so on (GEM).

TONE CONTROL

The amplifier of your home stereo has bass and treble controls that allow you to adjust the 'timbre' of the sound by boosting or cutting low and high frequency ranges. This is known as *equalization* or *EQ*. Most digital keyboard instruments have similar controls.

Switch or fader

Lower priced pianos often have a brilliance switch with the settings *mellow* (reduced highs, boosted lows), *normal*, and *bright* (boosted highs, reduced lows). A continuously adjustable brilliance control with a fader or up-down buttons allows for finer adjustment.

Graphic equalizer

Another step up is a tone control with separate controls for a number of frequency ranges or *bands*. This is known as a *graphic equalizer*. It graphically shows you its settings. Graphic EQs are usually limited to mid- and pro-level instruments.

Bass boost

Dance music often requires a fat, pumping bass sound,

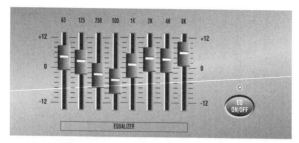

An 8-band graphic equalizer. The band marked 63 (63 hertz) controls the lowest frequencies; the band marked 8K (8,000 hertz) controls the highest frequencies.

which some companies supply with features labeled *auto loudness* or *bass boost*, for example.

Effect

Equalizers are usually considered effects: They affect the timbre of the sound you produce. Other effects are covered on pages 60–65.

TUNING

Digital keyboard instruments don't need to be tuned before you can play. However, you can adjust their tuning in various ways.

Fine tuning   Tipcode KEYS-009

When you're playing in a band or along to a CD, your instrument may sound a little *flat* (too low) or *sharp* (too high). To adjust this, most keyboards and pianos can be fine-tuned. Usually, your keyboard will be tuned at the standard pitch A=440. This means that the key A4 (see page 27) produces a pitch of 440 vibrations per second, or 440 hertz. When you play this pitch on a guitar or a violin, the string will vibrate 440 times per second.

Increments

Most instruments can be tuned at least a quarter tone up and down (+ or – 50 cents), and some can be tuned as much as a half tone up (to A=466) and down (A=415). Increments of 1 hertz are acceptable; the smallest increments are 0.1 hertz. Finetuning is also known as *master tuning*.

Fine tuning the instrument in 0.5 hertz increments.

Quarter-tone intervals

When you go from one key to the next, you play *half-tone* or *semitone* intervals. In various non-Western styles of music, though, smaller, quarter-tone intervals are common. Some instruments have preset tunings for these styles of music, in which, for example, D and A or E and B are lowered a quarter tone. Others have even more sophisticated features that allow you to play any type of scale with similar *microtunings*.

Historical tunings

In Western music, several different tunings or *temperaments* have been used over the centuries. If you want to play the music of a certain era, it helps if you can play it with the proper tuning.

Your choice

Some instruments offer a choice of tunings for this purpose, from the thirteenth-century Pythagorean tuning to the eighteenth-century Kirnberger or Tartini Valotti, as well as different modern piano tunings. One example would be *stretch tuning*, which compensates the perception that high notes sound too low (so they're tuned up a bit), and low notes sound too high (so they're tuned a little flat).

Personal tunings

Two identical, perfectly tuned acoustic pianos can sound very different because of minute differences in the exact way they have been tuned. Some digital pianos can be tuned per key, so you can have your favorite piano tuner tune it for you the way you like it.

TRANSPOSING

If the vocalist of the band can't sing the highest notes, you will have to play the entire song a number of steps lower. In other words,

Transposing: In the position shown, each C key sounds the note D; each D key sounds the note E, and so on.

you need to *transpose* the song to *another key**. On acoustic instruments, this means that you'll have to use different keys, chords, or fingerings. On a digital instrument, you can simply use the transpose function. This makes all the keys sound any number of half steps higher or lower, and you can just play the chords you're used to.

One or two octaves

Keyboards and pianos can often be transposed over a range of one or two octaves, sometimes even more. This feature also increases the range of your instrument: You can play higher and lower notes than the actual number of keys suggests. A tip: When you use the split function, you can usually independently transpose each section.

Transposing and layers

If you can transpose one of the voices in a layered sound, you can play two-voiced harmonies using single keys only – a piano with a layered organ voice that sounds an octave higher, for example.

POLYPHONY AND MULTITIMBRALITY

Early electronic instruments were *monophonic*: As with a sax or a trumpet, you could produce only a single (*mono*) note at a time. All modern keyboard instruments are *polyphonic*, so you can play a lot of notes simultaneously, like you can on a guitar or a piano. Most are also *multitimbral*, meaning they can produce multiple sounds (*timbres*) at once.

Polyphony

For most applications, you will need an instrument with at least *24-note* or *24-voice* polyphony. Why, if you have

Tipbook Music on Paper tells you everything about key signatures and transposing.

ten fingers only? Because the accompaniment plays a lot of simultaneous notes too, for one thing. And when you use layered sounds, each note will use up as many voices as there are layers.

On piano
On a piano you need multinote polyphony to play sustained chords, or *arpeggios* (broken chords) and glissandos with the damper pedal in order to sound dozens of notes simultaneously. Beginning and intermediate pianists need 16- or 32-note polyphony at least, but professional pianos often have 64- or 128-note polyphony, or even more. Low polyphony can cause 'note stealing' (notes being cut off when you play another note) or 'attack flamming.'

Multitimbral
A *16-part multitimbral* instrument is capable of having sixteen *different* sounds or voices going on at the same time. This may seem like a lot, but splits, layers, and accompaniments may eat up these parts faster than you think.

REGISTRATION MEMORIES
On most instruments you can save your settings for each song (style, sounds, effects, transposition, tempo, volume levels, etc.) in *registration memories, registrations, panel storage settings, performance settings,* or *user programs.* These can be recalled at the touch of a button. Their number varies from four or six to a hundred or more.

Pre-programmed settings
Some instruments have pre-programmed settings for hundreds of well-known songs. To prevent copyright problems, song titles may have been changed slightly (e.g., *Against All 'The' Odds*).

Registration memories.

SEQUENCERS
A basic sequencer allows you to record just one or a few

songs that you can play back – and that's it. A really powerful sequencer is almost like a digital recording studio that allows you to create multipart songs, recording each new instrument while playing back the ones you've already recorded.

No sound...
Sequencers do not record sound (like cassette or MD records do), but they digitally record the keys you press, the velocity at which you do that, the effects you use, the pedals you press, and so on.

... but events
Everything you do during a performance (pressing a key, releasing the key, setting the intensity of an effect, setting the tempo, using a pedal) is an *event*. A sequencer records these events as *MIDI messages* (see page 99). Playing back these data is like having a remote control operate the instrument.

Number of events
The capacity of a sequencer is usually expressed as the number of events it can hold in memory, and sometimes as the number of notes. A '1,600-note song memory' may sound impressive at first, but at a moderate tempo you play that many notes in a matter of minutes. For digital pianos, a capacity of 30,000 to 45,000 events is not unusual. Because they have to record the accompaniment parts as well, keyboards need larger memories. Top level keyboards may go up to 250,000 events or more. In some cases, their song memory can be expanded.

Number of songs or measures
Sequencers also vary in the number of songs they can hold, ranging from one to 200 or more. Some companies also specify the maximum number of bars or measures for each song. Here's a guideline: At tempo 120 a five-minute song in $\frac{4}{4}$ has 150 bars.

Disk drives
The sequencer's memory limitations are hardly relevant when your instrument allows you to store data on floppy disks or any other type of media (see pages 67–68).

Number of tracks

Very basic sequencers have one single track. You play, it records: end of story. If you have two tracks, you can usually play one back while recording the other. This allows you to record the left hand part first, for example, and then add the right hand part to it on the second track.

Multitracking

The more tracks you have, the more complicated you can make your arrangements, through *multitracking*. Many instruments have an eight-track sequencer, while top-of-the-line models often sport 16 or 32 tracks, allowing you to add as many parts, sound by sound, part by part. A few instruments have dual sequencers that can be synchronized, so you can use all their tracks simultaneously.

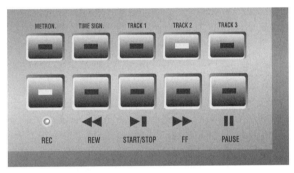

A three-track sequencer with the familiar transport controls.

Resolution

Sequencers record events according to a grid. The finer this grid, the more accurately the sequencer will reproduce the exact timing of your notes. This grid is referred to as the instrument's (*timing*) *resolution*. With a resolution of 48, there are 48 different points at which a note can be recorded within each beat (usually a quarter note). This isn't as accurate as it may sound. If you want a true representation of your playing, the sequencer should have a resolution of 96 or 192 *ppq* (*pulses per quarter note*).

Quantizing

Sophisticated sequencers allow you to fix timing errors in your performance. This is known as *quantizing* or *quantization*. If you set the quantization to sixteenth notes,

every poorly timed note you play will be moved to the nearest sixteenth note.

(Non-)volatile

Sequencers in entry-level instruments may memorize and store your performance only until the instrument is switched off. Most sequencers preserve their contents at power-off, however: They have a *non-volatile* song memory.

Editing

The degree to which a sequencer allows you to edit your recordings varies per instrument. On some, you can just change the playback tempo. On others, you may also be able to correct wrong notes, replace sounds, change the effect settings or EQ per sound, transpose the sequence, copy and paste parts of the song, layer sounds – and so on.

Real time, step time

Most sequencers can record both in *real time* (you play, the sequencer records) and in *step time*. Step time recording is rather like programming, and it's usually a lot more complicated than real time recording – but it does allow you to record things you can't actually play…

Your computer

If your instrument's sequencer isn't powerful enough, you can hook up your instrument to your computer and get a *software sequencer*: a piece of software that turns your computer into a sequencer. Software sequencers or *computer-based sequencers* usually have numerous editing options, and they allow you to store as many songs as you like. Most of these sequencers can record audio too, so you can add vocals and actual instruments to your recordings, which can then be burned onto CD-R discs.

STANDARD MIDI FILES

If you save a performance on disk, it will commonly be stored as a *standard MIDI file*, also known as *MIDI file* or *SMF*.

Formats

Depending on the instrument, the sequencer will use a

certain SMF format. These formats (GM, GS, XG, and others) are briefly explained on pages 106–107. They make sure that if you play back your performance on an instrument that can handle that format, you will hear the same voices you played when recording the song, with the same effects and edits,

General MIDI

The GM (General MIDI) format is the only one that can be read and saved by most sequencers. As a result, Standard MIDI files are often dubbed General MIDI files.

Disk drive

MIDI files take up very little storage space: A song is usually no larger than 40K to 100K. (A CD-quality audio recording takes up about 10MB – 10,000K – per minute!) As MIDI files are that small, you can save a lot of 'music' on a 3.5" floppy disk. This explains why this type of disk has been a popular storage medium among keyboard players for so long.

Songs

Most popular songs are available as Standard MIDI files, either commercially or free. They can be purchased on floppy disks or downloaded from the Internet. You can use these songs to sing along to, to provide accompaniment for your solos, to practice playing them, or to just play back and enjoy… If you want to sing along it can be helpful if your keyboard is capable of transposing the song to a key that matches your range (see page 53).

Arranging and editing MIDI files

Provided that you have the right software, you can edit Standard MIDI files on your computer: change voices, effect levels, or velocities, transpose the song, and so on. Some keyboards allow you to arrange song files on the fly, so you can *loop* (endlessly repeat) the chorus as long as everybody's still dancing, for example.

Files and styles

Some keyboards can combine Standard MIDI files with any style you want, so you can experiment and see which styles best fit your favorite songs.

Various types

There are various types of Standard MIDI files: Type 0, Type 1, Type 2, and Type 1+lyrics.

- Type 0 saves songs in a single track. As each part uses its own MIDI channel (see page100), you can still edit the individual parts, provided you have the right equipment.
- Type 1 uses a multitrack format.
- Type 1+Lyrics can present the lyrics of the song on your display, if your instrument can handle this format.
- Type 2, which is rarely used, can save multiple songs in a single file.

Type 0

Some entry-level or older instruments can handle Type 0 only. Instruments that can read Type 1 can also read type 0. If you want to make sure that every instrument can read your MIDI files, save them as Type 0.

SAMPLERS

Sampling is a feature that's usually reserved for high-end keyboards. With a sampler, you can make digital recordings – samples – of sounds, and add them to the voices in your instrument's memory. A sample can be a single sound or note, or a short phrase, a guitar riff, a drum loop, or whatever, recorded by using the microphone or line inputs of your instrument (see Chapter 8).

Sample memory

The amount of sample memory determines the maximum length of a sample. As a guideline, a 16MB memory allows for a stereo sample of slightly under 90 seconds. Sample memory can usually be expanded with SIMM memory modules, similar to the way you can have the internal memory of your computer expanded.

Sample formats

Samples are commonly saved as WAV files (for PC) or AIFF files (for Macintosh), so you can edit them on your computer. WAV and AIFF are not the only sample formats. Some companies such as Akai, Korg, and Kurzweil (see Chapter 14) have proprietary formats. Note that samplers can't always read all formats.

Good samples

The digital quality of a sample or digital recording is expressed in bits and kHz (kilohertz). Higher figures indicate a better sample quality.

Bit depth and sampling rate

A regular audio CD is 'sampled' at 16-bit/44.1 kHz. A lower *bit depth*, expressed in a number of bits, will make the sample less dynamic, which reduces differences between soft and loud and increases hiss. A lower *sampling rate* (expressed in kHz) will make for duller, poorer, and less natural sounding samples – but the file size will be smaller. For your reference, an 8-bit/11kHz sample sounds about as bad as an answering machine. Many high-end instruments use 24-bit/96 kHz sampling.

Sample editing

Sampling is more than just making a digital recording of a sound. It also involves editing. Samplers offer various editing options, such as *truncate* (cut off everything you don't need), *loop* (make a long sound based on a shorter sample), *normalize* (equalize the loudness of various samples), *reverse*, *slice* (cut them into pieces that can then be triggered separately), and so on.

EFFECTS

All but some entry-level instruments have one or more effects to enhance your performance.

Reverb   Tipcode KEYS-010

Reverb, the most common effect, creates a sense of *ambience*. It makes music sound as if it's being played in a concert hall, rather than at home. Many instruments have various types of reverb to choose from (*e.g.*, concert hall, room, church). You can usually adjust the amount or the length of the reverb too. Reverb is also a *master* effect: It's commonly used on all the instruments in the mix – accompaniment tracks, melody, and vocals.

Chorus   Tipcode KEYS-010

Chorus is another popular effect. The added fullness, presence, character, and spaciousness of a chorus work great

for electric pianos, strings, guitar accompaniments, and pad sounds (see page 73). Many instruments provide various types of chorus, up to twenty or more.

Digital signal processor

The effects in digital instruments are generated and controlled by one or more *digital signal processors* (*DSP*). If an instrument has just one DSP, you can commonly use just one effect at the time. With two DSPs, you're a lot more flexible: You can use reverb over the entire mix and add a little chorus on your electric piano sound, for example.

More DSPs

Higher-level instruments often have one DSP for reverb effects, one for chorus effects, and one or more for other effects. Keyboards with a microphone input often have a dedicated DSP for vocal effects.

Number of effects

The number of effects may vary from one to a hundred or more, with various types of each effect, effect combinations, and with both preset and user-definable effects.

Effects

Tipcode KEYS-010

Chorus and reverb are just two of the many effects you can come across. Here are some of the others:

- *Flangers* and *phasers* offer two variations on the chorus effect. A phaser makes for a sweeping or swirling effect, and flanging adds anything between a departing jet plane and a slight, metallic, sweeping edge to the sound. Flangers, phasers, and choruses are the best-known *modulation effects*.
- A *delay* or *echo* repeats the note you've just played. A short delay, repeating the note a split second after you played it, makes the sound a little fatter (*doubling*). Long delay times allow you to play along with the echoed notes. Delay, echo, and reverb are known as *ambient effects*.
- *Overdrive* and *distortion* emulate the effect of overdriving an amplifier, which makes the sound literally distort. Overdrive is the milder one of the two. Electric rock and blues guitarists can't do without these effects, which are very effective on organs and electric pianos too.
- An *enhancer* makes for a brighter, tighter, more sparkling,

and cleaner sound with additional presence and detail.

- *Tremolo* rhythmically varies the sound's volume (*amplitude modulation*). Works well on electric pianos.
- *Rotor* or *rotary* are two of the many terms that indicate an digital emulation of a Leslie speaker (see page 117), which literally swirls the sound around. This effect can usually be set at two speeds – *chorale* (slow) and *tremolo* (high).

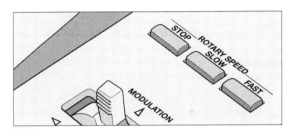

Setting the speed of a rotary effect.

- *Ping-pong* sends the first note to the right speaker, the following note to the left speaker, and so on.
- *Panning, panorama,* or *pan* is a control you also find on mixing boards, allowing you to position an instrument in the stereo mix anywhere from far left to far right. *Auto pan* makes the sound smoothly move from left to right.
- A *wah-wah* does exactly what the name sounds like. With an *auto-wah*, the effect level is controlled by how loud you play.
- The effect of a *ring modulator* is usually described as a weird, clanking, bell-like, or gong-like sound. Commonly used on organs and electric pianos.
- *Lo-fi,* the opposite of hi-fi, makes the instrument sound as if it's played through a vintage, beaten-up portable radio.
- A *compressor* reduces dynamic differences, boosting soft notes and reducing the ones that are too loud. It can also be used to make (electric guitar!) notes sustain for a long period of time.
- *Amp simulators* and *cabinet simulators* are increasingly popular, especially among guitarists and bassists. They emulate the sound of popular amplifiers and speaker cabinets.
- *EQ* (see pages 50–51) is usually considered an effect too.

Harmonies

Harmony or *auto harmonize* are two of the many names for an effect that creates harmonies by adding one or more extra notes to the notes that you play, so you hear two, three, or more pitches instead of one. The chords that you play are taken into account, preventing inappropriate notes: If you play a C-minor chord (C, E♭, G) with your left hand, the effect will add an E♭ rather than an E to your solo part.

Harmony types
Tipcode KEYS-011

Even entry-level instruments sometimes offer several types of harmony to choose from. One will add a note an octave above the note you're playing; another will add a third (major or minor, depending on the chord you're playing) or a fifth above, or the third and fifth step of a chord, sounding either above or below the note you're play-ing, and so on. Some of these harmony types fit a certain style of music (*e.g.*, big band or country); others are meant to enhance certain sounds, such as string ensembles.

Arpeggiator
Tipcode KEYS-012

An *arpeggiator* is another effect that helps create the impression that you're doing more than you really are. When you play a chord, an arpeggiator makes it sound as though you're playing the notes involved – and a number of related notes – in a (usually) fast, repetitive sequence. Arpeggio literally means 'broken chord.' Arpeggiators are a common feature on synths and workstations, but you may find them on some keyboards too.

Tweaking effects

You can often tweak any of the built-in effects to your liking. The more elements you can adjust and the more precisely you can adjust them, the more musical use the effects will generally have.

Depth, rate, level
Tipcode KEYS-013

One clear example would be a chorus, which may have two or more *parameters*. The effect's *depth* sets the depth of the chorus 'waves.' With *rate* you control the tempo of the waves. *Mix level* adjusts how much of the chorus effect you hear and how much of the original, clean sound.

Vibrato

Vibrato has similar parameters: the depth and speed of the pitch variation, and the *delay time* (how long it lasts before vibrato sets in). On less sophisticated instruments, you may be able to set only the intensity of an effect (*e.g.*, light, normal, and deep) – or not even that.

Considerations

Here are some additional points to consider when looking at effects sections:

- If you can control effect settings in **real time**, you can adjust things on the spot rather than being required to go through a couple of menus to adjust your delay, for example.
- It makes things much more musical if you can **adjust the tempo** (rate) of a delay or a tremolo to the tempo of the song, preferably with a tap tempo control: You simply tap the desired tempo, and the effect follows.
- It's also good to be able to **independently adjust the levels** of the selected effects for the various voices in layered sounds, for example.
- If you don't want to remember and recreate your effect settings every time you play, you need an instrument with **user presets**, which allow you to store and recall things.
- On some instruments, you can make **effect combinations**. If you connect two effects *in series*, the first effect will be processed by the second. Possible combinations are overdrive and flanger or delay; distortion and chorus, flanger, or delay; or chorus and delay. If you're connecting effects in *parallel* (chorus and flanger, for example), the two effects do not influence each other.

Judging effects

To properly judge effects, you need to know how to use them. Using effects is like using spices when cooking: Adding a bit of flanging can work great, but overdoing it may ruin the sound. And chorus is great for electric piano voices, but it makes acoustic pianos sound terribly out of tune – which, in certain situations, may be exactly what you want to do. Note that the quality and character of the available effects vary per brand and per instrument: Digital distortions can sound just right (warm and fat), or

way too edgy or harsh; reverbs can be clean and crisp, or so muddy and soggy that you loose detail – and so on.

VOCAL PROCESSORS

Instruments with a microphone input often have a separate vocal processor, which features various effects dedicated to vocal performance.

Harmonies

You can usually add harmonies to your voice, so you can create a virtual chorus or add backing vocals to your songs. Depending on the specifications of the instrument, you may be able to make your voice sound like a trio or a quartet; a male choir, a female choir, or a children's choir; close-harmony or Andrew Sisters-style...

Some other features

A *gender* function or *voice transformer* can make a male voice sound female, or vice versa. Likewise, you can make your voice sound like a baby, a rapper, or an alien. A *vocoder* makes your voice sound synthetic or robot-like. A few instruments feature *auto-tune*, a device that automatically tunes your notes to sound the correct pitch. A more common feature is a button that switches the vocal processor off, so you can address your audience in-between songs without the effects you use for singing. A *vocal remover* or *voice killer* removes the solo singing voice of prerecorded songs, so you can sing along yourself.

Karaoke

That said, some keyboards can double as karaoke machines, showing the lyrics on the display or an external monitor. Karaoke song files are available in stores and on the Internet.

SYNTHESIS OPTIONS

Keyboards with one or more synthesis options let you alter or edit your sounds, though usually less extensively than dedicated synthesizers will. You can give sounds smoother or sharper attacks or rounder or more angular 'shapes,' change their timbre through time, and so on.

Envelope generator

Tipcode KEYS-014

An *envelope generator* sets the 'contour' of a sound. The four parameters of an envelope generator are attack, decay, sustain, and release (ADSR).

- *Attack* is the time a sound takes to reach its maximum volume level. *Decay* is the time it takes the sound to drop to its *sustain* level, *i.e.*, the level at which a sound continues while holding the key down.
- *Release* is how long the sound continues after releasing the key.

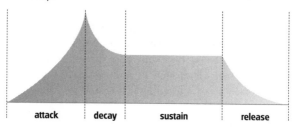

attack   decay   sustain   release

Filters

Tipcode KEYS-015

A few keyboards have filters that you can use to let certain frequencies pass, while cutting off others; this allows you to alter sounds dramatically. A *low pass filter* cuts off the frequencies above a specific point (the *cut-off frequency*, which may be adjustable); a *high pass filter* cuts off the frequencies below a certain point. A *band pass filter* lets you control the frequencies that can pass the filter unaffected, while cutting off other frequencies. 'Real' synthesizers usually provide you with various very flexible filter types.

LFO

An *LFO* (*low frequency oscillator*) is an electronic device that produces a slow (low-frequency) 'wave' that can be used to rhythmically influence the volume (*i.e.*, tremolo), pitch (vibrato), or timbre (wah-wah) of a sound. On a few keyboards, you can set the intensity, rate, and delay of the LFO. Real synthesizers offer a lot more options, such as the choice of different waveforms, each of which has a different effect on the sound. Suppose you use an LFO to influence volume: A *square wave* would mean the volume is continuously switched on and off abruptly, while a *sawtooth wave* would make it swell gradually and end abruptly, just like the shape of a sawtooth suggests.

DISK DRIVES AND OTHER MEDIA

Many keyboard instruments have a floppy disk drive built in, or they provide access for other types of storage media such as media cards. With these media, there's no end to the number of songs, styles, performance settings, and other data you would want to store. You can also use them to load new songs, sounds (samples), accompaniments, and other data into your instrument.

Floppy disk

For many years, the 3.5" 1.44 MB floppy disk has been one of the most common media to store data for musical instruments. Both the disks and the drives are cheap, and MIDI files take up little space. However, the disks themselves are not extremely reliable, so always make backups and bring them along for a performance.

More

On some instruments, floppy disks can be formatted to hold more data (1.6MB) than usual. These expanded disks are, however, usually unreadable by other instruments.

A built-in floppy disk drive.

Faster

It can take a little time for a floppy disk drive to access the information on disk. That's why many instruments allow you to keep playing while loading data from disk (*multitasking*). Some companies have found other ways to reduce access time, known by proprietary names such as *disk direct, direct play,* or *ultra quick start.*

Hard disks

Onboard hard disks are faster than floppies, and they provide immediate access to songs, styles, and other data.

Some instruments come with a hard disk that's pre-loaded with hundreds of songs, styles, and sounds, so you can start using them right away.

Small

Hard disks in instruments are usually much smaller than the ones used in computers. When 40GB hard drives were common in computers, instruments often came with 4 or 6GB models – which still can be big enough, provided you don't want to use it to store loads of space-hungry WAV files (*i.e.*, audio samples). Some instruments have a connection for an external hard disk (see page 97).

Other storage media

Most storage media that are introduced for computer, find their way to musical instruments as well, from the (now obsolete) ZIP and JAZ disks to PCMCIA cards, SmartMedia cards, CompactFlash cards, SD cards, and other universal data cards. These cards are road tough (no moving parts) and small (some no larger than a postage stamp). They also provide instant access to their data, so you can use them in real time. Their capacity varies from a couple of megabytes to several gigabytes, and more in the future.

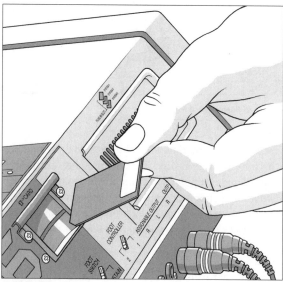

SmartMedia card.

CD burner
An integrated CD burner lets you store audio files (WAV) and MP3 files, and back up your own styles, registrations, sounds, and so on.

Formats
To be able to use data that are stored on a particular medium, you need to have the right hardware, and your instrument needs to be able to read the format in which the data are stored. Next to a small number of generic formats (SMF, WAV, MP3, and so on) there are dozens of proprietary formats. Some companies make instruments that can handle all or most of these formats; others offer limited compatibility.

JUST LIKE COMPUTERS
Despite their appearance most electronic musical instruments are essentially computers that produce sound.

Operating system
Just like computers, they have an operating system (OS). Many companies let you update the operating system either with disks or via the Internet. Just like new software for your computer, an update may provide you with new functions and features, or just with a better, bug-free instrument. These updates are usually free of charge.

New sounds and songs
Likewise, many companies offer new sounds, songs, drum sets, and styles on the Internet. You can use a floppy disk to transport files from your computer to your instrument, just like you can move files from one computer to the next, but it is easier if you can hook the two of them up: See Chapters 8 and 9 for more information.

Hardware expansion
Synthesizers and workstations can often be expanded with new hardware – which, by the time you read this, may have become more widespread as an option for keyboards and digital pianos too. Companies market *expansion boards* that offer anything from sampling to extra sounds (*wave expansion boards*), a SCSI interface (see page 97), a video

interface (see page 43), an arpeggiator, extra synthesizer power with added polyphony or effect processors, various tone generators, and so on.

EDUCATIONAL FEATURES

Though they can't replace a real teacher, the educational features that some instruments offer can make it easier to get started, make practicing more effective, or help you expand your knowledge.

One hand at a time

One very common way to use your keyboard as a practicing tool was mentioned on page 20: You can play back the (pre-) recorded left or right hand part and play along with your other hand, so you practice one hand at the time. Some instruments have a hundred or more pre-recorded songs available that can be played back one hand at a time.

Tempo

It helps if you can set the tempo, so you can either record a piece slowly and play it back at the intended speed, or slow a recording down so you can play along. With a *phrase trainer*, you can select a section of the song and play it back until you master it.

Modes

More advanced systems also offer other ways to learn pre-recorded songs, often providing various modes. One mode lets you concentrate on your timing of the notes; no matter which key you play, it will always produce the right pitch (*any key play* or *timing mode*). A second mode is about playing the correct melody note; the left hand part or the accompaniment will wait until you have played it (*waiting mode*). In a third mode you need to play the required notes in time, using the right keys. At the end of the song, a computerized voice may tell you how well you did. The instrument may even grade your work to help you keep track of your progress.

Which key?

Some instruments tell you which keys to play, either by indicating them on the display, or by using *lighted keys*:

You simply play the keys that light up. Dual lighting systems use different colors for the left and right hand parts. The correct fingering may be displayed too (1 is your thumb, 2 your index finger, etc.), or a digital voice may tell you which finger to use for the next note. Some keyboards count the beats out loud ('*One, Two, Three; One, Two, Three…*') or tell you the name of the note you're supposed to play (C, D, E, etc).

Chords
Additionally, an instrument may be able to help you figure out chords. Or you can play your pre-programmed chords by pressing any key in the lower section, so you can focus on the melody or your solo. Some instruments even offer guidance in advanced subjects like counterpoint and harmony.

Games
Musical keyboard games come in many variations: The instrument sounds a note or a chord, and you have to guess which one it was; it plays a rhythmical pattern, which you have to repeat – and so on.

USER'S MANUAL
Keyboards and most digital pianos offer more than you may be able to find out by yourself. Even for advanced players, a user's manual is usually indispensable.

Cover to cover
Reading the manual from cover to cover is a lot of work, but it will tell you everything the instrument is capable of and where to find things for future reference. Unfortunately, manuals often have an incomplete index, making it hard to re-find specific information without having to go through the entire book again.

6. SOUND

An instrument may have a thousand features – but first and foremost, you should like the way it sounds. This chapter explains the various types of sounds, sound quality, methods for judging sounds, and built-in and external amplification.

If you use a digital piano to play classical or jazz piano music, you may be perfectly happy if it has just one good, dynamic piano sound. But if you want to be a one-man band, or use a keyboard to arrange music for a band or a larger group of musicians, you're better off with an instrument that provides you with a thousand-plus sounds.

Budget and sound

More money usually buys you more sounds. Entry-level keyboards often have a hundred sounds or more, while mid- and pro-level instruments may offer over a thousand different voices.

On digital pianos, the number of sounds usually varies between a handful on the least expensive models to forty or more on higher-level instruments. However, price differences don't reflect the number of sounds as much as their quality.

Three basic categories

The sounds on a typical keyboard fall into three basic categories: samples of acoustic instruments, samples of 'artificial' synthesizer sounds, and samples of sound effects such as ringing phones and gunshots. The acoustic instruments are the largest group.

Shamisen

The names of the 'acoustic' voices are usually self-explanatory, but a little knowledge makes it easier to choose the right sounds for your performance: You may never use the subtle sound of a *shamisen* in a song if you have no idea what a shamisen is... Or you may do a lot of work to combine the voices of two violins, a viola, and a cello, because you didn't know that you have a built-in 'string quartet' that produces exactly that.

Synthesizer and pad sounds   Tipcode KEYS-016

Keyboards also provide a selection of synthesizer sounds, using more or less descriptive names such as techno, funky lead, adrenaline, and attack saw... Pad sounds are synthetic, dream-like sounds with a slow attack, sporting names like space voice, halo pad, fantasia, or dark moon.

Style-related sounds

Some instruments also have groups of sounds for certain musical styles, such as techno or R&B, or they have special DJ sounds on board.

Drum sets

Keyboards and ensemble pianos offer various types of drum sets to meet your needs: A heavy metal act requires different sounding drums than a jazz tune or a rap song. Keyboards usually have a choice of standard drum sets ('regular' sounding drums), one or more brush sets for jazz ballads, Cuban and Latin sets with congas, bongos, and other hand percussion instruments, electronic or synth sets for dance music, and so on. Some also feature symphonic percussion (timpani, symphonic cymbals, concert toms, etc.), African sets (talking drums, djembe, bougarabou, etc.), or other ethnic percussion sets.

Manual drums

Most keyboards can be used as a drum machine too: If you hit a button labeled *drums* or *m(anual) drums*, or if you select the 'drums' voice, you can play the instrument's drum and percussion sounds with the keys. When choosing an instrument, compare the drum sounds of various models and brands carefully to see which sounds would work best for your music and your taste.

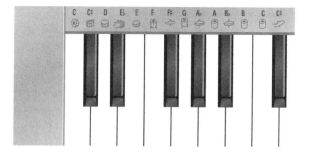

On many keyboards, small icons tell you which keys trigger which percussion instruments.

Special attention

Pay special attention to the bass drum and snare drum sounds (you're bound to use these drums more than others) and to the cymbal sounds: Cymbals are extremely hard to sample. The various percussion instruments are usually triggered by the same keys on different instruments: the ride cymbal by key E♭4, the snare drum by key D3, and so on.

Two samples

Some instruments have different samples under one key: a regular timbale sound when played not too loud, and a timbale rimshot when you hit the same key harder, for example.

GOOD SOUNDS

Judging sounds is mainly a matter of taste: You may like one piano sound better than the other, of course, even though the other has better technical specifications. Even so, some information on how sound quality is determined can make it easier to find the instrument you like best.

Not like you   Tipcode KEYS-017

If you play higher and lower notes on an acoustic instrument, it isn't only the pitch that changes: The sound gets a different timbre too. If you record a note played on a piano and play it back at double the speed, it will sound an octave higher – but it doesn't sound much like a piano anymore. If you record yourself singing a note and you play it back an octave higher, it doesn't sound like you

anymore. So for a sampled instrument to sound realistic at various pitches, it needs to have been sampled at various pitches.

One or more per octave

On low cost instruments, there may be no more than a single sample per octave: With a five-octave keyboard, that would add up to five grand piano samples, five tenor saxophone samples, and so on. However, to make a voice sound anything like the real thing, one sample per key is the minimum.

More per key

To have a sampled instrument sound even more natural, you need various samples per key. Why? Because playing an instrument louder also changes the timbre of the sound: It gets brighter, usually, and the attack may get more aggressive, and there will be more sustain...

Filters or samples

This effect can be imitated, to a certain extent, by using filters that let more high frequencies pass as you play louder. This makes for a more natural sound, but it's still not as good as playing and recording each note at various volume levels. On high-quality instruments, there may be three, four, or more samples per note.

From one to the next

When you play increasingly louder, the instrument should go from one sample to the next without you hearing that it does. Various techniques (e.g., *velocity crossfade* and *physical modeling*; see page 76) are used to make this a smooth process, just like it is with an acoustical instrument.

Rates

The bit depth and sampling rate of the samples (see page 60) give an indication of their quality, but these figure are usually not provided with the instrument.

Stereo

Stereo samples will make a digital piano sound natural by adding depth and dimension to the sound. A stereo sample takes up twice the amount of memory of a mono sample!

Long samples

The long sustaining sound of a low piano note requires a very long sample. It is cheaper to use a shorter sample and loop the sound, slowly decreasing the volume level. Looped samples usually don't sound as natural, though.

More memory

All the above features (more samples per key, stereo samples, long samples) require additional sample memory – and that's what raises the price. Some figures for your reference: Sample memory, often indicated as *Wave ROM*, may vary from 4MB for over 600 voices on a four hundred dollar keyboard, to 64MB or more for some 1,200 voices on a two thousand dollar instrument. Grand piano samples may take up much less than a megabyte on entry-level instruments and more than 80MB on a high-quality digital piano – and in the year 2000, a piano that uses more than 5GB for its grand piano voice was introduced.

Sound improvement

There are many more ways improve sound quality on a digital instrument – adding vibrato, for example, or including some of the mechanical sounds that acoustic instruments make, like fret sounds or squeaking strings on guitars. Some companies use a lot of reverb to hide the lower quality of their samples. A lot of reverb may sound impressive at first, but it gets tiresome after a while.

Technology

Physical modeling offers another means to enhance these sounds. This involves using computer models to emulate characteristics of acoustic instruments, such as the sizes and weights of hammers in a grand piano, the mass of the tone bar or the location of the pickup in an electric piano, the resonance of the piano strings when the damper pedal is used (*sympathetic resonance*, by which undamped strings resonate along with the notes being played), the residual resonance of the piano's wooden casing and soundboard, and so on.

Tone wheel organ

Other popular sampled sounds may reflect just as much attention to details as the piano samples. For example,

samples of tone wheel organs (see page 117) may simulate the 'leakage' noise that comes from the tone wheels, or the click sound generated by older tone wheel organs whose contacts need cleaning.

PLAY-TESTING

Play-testing instruments to judge their sound is mainly a matter of comparing them. It's not easy to remember sounds in detail, so this is best done in one session. Remember, however, that your ears will need a break before you think they do. So take five, now and then, or go home and return the next day.

One at a time

Compare one type of sound at a time, and concentrate on the sounds you're likely to use most. Select the best piano sound on each instrument and compare those sounds. Do the same with the organs, various string sounds, electric and acoustic guitars, and so on.

Choose the right instruments

Some instruments have great electric guitar sounds and mediocre acoustic guitar voices. Some have great saxophones but disappointing brass sections. You can ask a sales person to offer recommendations based on the sounds you're commonly using.

Jazz or classical

It's good to know which type of sound fits the music you play. If you play classical piano music only, you'll need a piano sound that offers plenty of dynamics and nuance; a piano in a rock band should sound a lot brighter, with more attack, while dynamics are less important.

An expensive one

Even if you're looking for a low-budget or mid-price instrument, it may be good to include some really expensive ones in your search: Their sounds set a standard that you can aim for. Likewise, even if you plan to buy a keyboard, it can be good to listen to the piano voices of a digital piano. You can also listen to some acoustic pianos first, of course.

How to play it

Even the very best sample of a saxophone or a violin won't *sound* anywhere near the real thing if you don't *play* it as you would play the real thing. In other words: You shouldn't play typical keyboard licks using a saxophone or guitar sound, for example. To emulate the sound of an instrument, you need to translate onto the keyboard the way that instrument is played: Different instruments require completely different keyboard technique. Likewise, you should judge sounds in their proper context. Have the keyboard play a rock accompaniment when judging rock guitar sounds, for example.

Harpsichords and Clavinets

It also helps to know about the character of the 'instruments' you are judging. A harpsichord is supposed to sound very classical (and lack dynamics!), while the vaguely related Clavinet is usually supposed to sound extremely funky.

The range

Try the main sounds throughout their range. Most sounds do very well in the middle of the keyboard, but do they get too harsh or too thin in the high range, or too muddy or indistinct in the low range? On lower quality instruments, voices tend to sound acceptable within a very small range only.

The natural range

Remember that 'real' instruments have limited ranges. You can't expect a bass sample to still sound like a bass if you play it above the instrument's natural range, or choir samples to sound like anything human if you play them at the extreme ends of the keyboard.

Words

Musicians often use very subjective words to describe what they're hearing: What one finds shrill (and so not attractive) another may describe as bright (and so not unattractive). Still, using such words can make it easier to find what you're looking for: It's more effective if you know that you want a transparent, colorful sound with bright highs and strong mids, rather than just a 'great' sound.

Miscellaneous tips

- Listen to **how sensitive** the sounds are to variations in touch. Classical pianists should pay special attention to the pedals too.
- When comparing specific voices on various instruments, make sure you set their **volumes to equal levels**.
- Compare sounds **without using effects** – and compare effects separately.
- Organs, synth sounds, flutes, and drum sounds are relatively **easy to sample**, so they will usually sound good. Pianos, guitars, saxes, and cymbals are a lot harder to get right.
- **String sections** often sound more convincing than individual string instruments, such as violin and cello.
- If you will use the instrument for performances, let someone else play it so you can judge the sound **from a distance** – where your audience will be. You can also use the demo for this purpose.

Headphones

Decent quality headphones (starting at around eighty dollars) usually produce a better sound quality than the built-in speakers. If you intend to use external amplification, auditioning the instrument via phones will give you a more honest impression of how good the sounds really are: Headphones exclude the performance of the onboard speakers and amplification, so they help to judge the quality of the samples on various instruments.

The lowest notes

When you're play-testing instruments using their built-in speakers, you might not be able to get the lowest notes to sound as loudly and clearly as the high ones. With their limited dimensions (and often enough, a limited price), these speakers are often unable to truly reproduce these low frequencies. If possible, hook the instrument up to an external sound system; the response is supposed to be even at all pitches, low to high.

The difference

If you have three saxophonists play the same saxophone, you'll hear three different timbres. Have one player play it, using different mouthpieces and different reeds, and you'll

hear a different timbre every time. Have the same player play a ballad on it, then a funky riff, and finally a classical phrase, and you'll hear three distinctly different voices coming from the same instrument – and so on. No matter how many features they have, digital instruments will probably never be that expressive. They do, however, offer possibilities that acoustic players can only dream of.

AMPLIFICATION: THE SPEAKERS

Any keyboard instrument's sound has a lot to do with the quality of its amplifier and speakers. Two remarks in advance:

- Many brands use the exact same samples for instruments in various price ranges. If so, the more expensive ones sound better simply because they have a better sound system.
- All keyboards and many digital pianos will benefit from an external sound system – especially if you take the instrument on the road.

Size

When it comes to speakers, size isn't everything. Some small ones are good, some large ones aren't.

Two or more

Most basic instruments have two speakers; one left, one right. More advanced models have separate speakers or *drivers* for the low range (*woofer*), and the mid-high ranges. This usually provides you with punchier basses, more pronounced mid-range frequencies, and brighter highs. In concentric speakers, the mid- or high-range driver is centered in the woofer, which can make the unit look as if it's only one speaker. Tip: The fact that an instrument has two speakers or two sets of speakers doesn't mean that all its sounds are stereo samples.

Four or more

Digital pianos – especially grand models – often have four or even more speakers to approximate the spatial characteristics of the acoustic instrument. In a six-speaker three-way system, you have two sets (stereo) of three (low, mid, high) speakers.

Speaker location

Keyboard speakers are usually mounted in the front panel, facing you directly. In digital pianos the speakers are mostly hidden. Some have separate *tweeters*, which produce the high frequencies, mounted above the keyboard, aiming the sound more toward your ears. A few instruments come with adjustable speakers.

Lows

In many styles of dance music, predominant lows are extremely important. That's why many keyboard speakers have bass-enhancing *ports*, and some even come with an (optional) subwoofer.

Hi-fi

The best way to judge speakers is to listen to them much as you would listen to a pair of hi-fi speakers. How's the balance between low end, midrange, and treble? Can they handle strong bass sounds and electric guitar stabs without distorting? Do you still hear a full, dynamic sound at low volume levels? A tip: Hit the demo button and listen from a distance. Remember, that's where your audience will be.

AMPLIFICATION: THE AMP

Good digital pianos usually have more powerful amplifiers than keyboards. The extra power is not to make the instrument sound louder, but to faithfully reproduce the dynamic range of an acoustic piano.

Figures

The power output of the stereo amplifiers in keyboards and low-budget digital pianos is usually somewhere between 2x5 and 2x15 watts (*i.e.*, 5 to 15 watts per channel). More expensive pianos have more powerful amps, with power ratings from some 30 to 100 or more watts per channel.

Bi-amping

Some instruments have separate, more powerful amps for the low frequencies, as true bass reproduction requires a lot of power. For example, a piano may have a 2x70 watt

amplifier for the low frequencies and a 2x30 watt amp for the mid and high range. This is known as *bi-amping*. Please note that there are companies that advertise such a combination as a '200 watt sound system' by simply adding up all those figures – but this is not how it works.

3D

To make instruments sound more spacious, they may feature *3D stereo enhancers*, *wide stereo* controls, and so on. Some can even be hooked up to a home theatre system for a surround sound playing experience.

EXTERNAL AMPLIFICATION

An external sound system will substantially improve the sound of most instruments. This should be no surprise, since a dedicated amplifier/speaker combination easily costs as much as a mid-price keyboard. The solutions offered in this chapter also work for speaker-less stage pianos.

Home stereo

You may try to improve the sound of your instrument by using your home stereo system instead of the built-in sound system. Do this only if you're sure that the stereo system can handle a keyboard instrument. Read the appropriate manuals first, as well as pages II and 93 of this book. Remember that you should *never* connect your keyboard instrument to the phono or disc input of your home sound system, as this input is designed to handle only the very weak signals from a record player. Instead, use one of the inputs marked *tape in*, *CD*, *aux*, or *tuner*.

Active speakers

Active speakers or *powered speakers* are often used in studios. They have built-in amplification, with either one or two (bi-amping) amps per speaker. They're usually better suited to amplify keyboards and pianos than your home stereo, and you can put them where they work best for you, rather than having to move your home stereo. Active speakers can also be used as a sound system in small venues – but they're usually not roadworthy and they're commonly designed to be used for listening at a close

range. (They're known as *nearfield* monitors.) Prices start around four to five hundred dollars for a set of two. Multimedia speakers are active speakers too. However, they're not intended for musical instrument amplification other than at very low volume levels (see page 95).

Keyboard amps

Alternatively you can get yourself one or two combo keyboard amplifiers. A combo amp is a single cabinet with an amp and usually two speakers – commonly a 10", 12", or 15" woofer, and a separate tweeter or horn for the high frequency ranges. Don't use guitar or bass amps; always go for dedicated keyboard combos.

Two

For a small venue, a keyboard combo with a 12" woofer and an amp that produces at least 60 watts should suffice. These generally start at around three or four hundred dollars. Note that you will probably want to buy two of them. After all, a single amp will not give you the stereo sound that your instrument is capable of; stereo will enhance most effects as well as your overall sound.

Mini-PA

Keyboard amps often have extra inputs for other instruments and/or microphones, an equalizer (see page 50), effect connectors, and one or more extra outputs. This

Combo keyboard amp (mono).

allows you to use them as miniature PA systems or as monitors. Price differences in amps with identical power ratings are usually due to the overall quality, the quality of the built-in speakers, and the available features.

Speakers off

When using an external sound system, you may still hear the instrument's onboard speakers. If you can't turn them off, or turn them down without reducing the overall output to zero, then plug your headphones in. It's even better to insert just the adaptor plug that usually comes with it: This prevents sound from leaking through the headphones. Some instruments have separate level controls for speakers and audio outs.

adaptor plug

Insert the adaptor plug of your headphones to turn off the onboard speakers.

7. ACCOMPANIMENTS

Just like a real band, the virtual band in a keyboard is supposed to make you – the soloist – sound good. This chapter introduces you to some of the details of auto-accompaniment sections, the way they sound, and their features.

The number of available styles on serious keyboards and ensemble pianos can vary from about sixty to a few hundred. Some offer two variations on each style, others as many as four, which helps to keep things interesting. After all, it can become a drag to hear the same country band play the same country groove in every country song.

More

The specified number of styles of an instrument is less important if you can edit them or create new ones yourself (see page 92), or if you can add new styles via the Internet, floppy disks, or other media. The number of available styles is staggering; you can find pretty much everything you need, from the latest dance beats to traditional Chinese styles.

Groups or families

Every keyboard manufacturer seems to have its own ideas on how to categorize styles. Hip-hop may be filed under 'contemporary' or 'dance,' for example, and big band under 'jazz' or 'swing.' Some companies use categories that contain the styles of a certain era (*e.g.*, fifties or sixties: rock, boogie, twist…) or a place (*e.g.*, European: polka, waltz, march…); others don't. Two more categories that you may

find on some instruments and not on others are 8-beat and 16-beat, referring to rock rhythms in which the drummer plays eighth or sixteenth notes respectively.

Focus

Likewise, some companies or individual instruments focus on 'traditional' styles such as jazz, rock, and Latin, while others are clearly dance oriented, with a focus on contemporary styles. Some also provide you with a large number of ethnic styles, while other have Western styles only.

Piano only

Many instruments have a number of pianist styles that replace the single notes you play with your left hand with an impressive piano accompaniment.

Comparing

Accompaniment sections are best judged style by style, concentrating on the ones you're most likely to use. Always compare styles at identical tempos and volume levels. (Styles usually have an assigned start-up tempo. This may be recalled automatically as soon as you select the style, or you may have to recall it by simultaneously pressing the +/- tempo buttons, for example.)

Musicians

Ideally, the various musical styles have been programmed by experts: Latin musicians for Latin rhythms, jazz musicians for jazz styles, rockers for rock styles. Though virtual bands will never be able to replace live bands, they can sound amazingly good. When comparing styles, listen to how natural or musical the band sounds. Some sound as mechanical as they are, while others really groove or swing. As the styles need to please a large group of customers, they're often more or less 'middle of the road.'

Sample grooves

A few instruments have additional sample grooves (audio recordings of guitar phrases, drum grooves, background vocals, etc.) onboard, which cannot be edited but can be combined with the common pre-programmed sequences. This enhances the feeling of playing live, with a real band.

Busy or relaxed

Some manufacturers go for very busy accompaniments, with a lot of drums and percussion, intricate bass lines, and complex chords, while others consistently prefer more sparse arrangements. Flashy accompaniments may sound impressive but may eventually become annoying.

Bare accompaniments

A tip: Start off by listening to only the bare accompaniments, without playing any chords. Then when you do hit a chord, you'll be able to tell how everything fits in together.

One by one

If you want to get the full picture of an instrument, then zap through the styles one by one. Don't forget to check out the ones you're unfamiliar with. They may inspire you to play things you've never even dreamt of.

THE BAND

Most styles, just like real life, provide you with a drummer and a bassist as a basic rhythm section. Next there will be one or more harmony instruments (piano, organ, or guitar, for example). On top of that you may hear strings, woodwinds, brass, or other melody instruments, and some percussion to spice things up. But how does this all actually work?

Number of tracks

Accompaniments have several tracks or parts, with each track dedicated to one or more 'members' or sections of the band.

The foundation

Often there is a track each for the drummer and the bass player, who lay down a foundation for the other musicians to build on. Drummers in particular can radically influence the sound and feel of a group, so make sure you like your drummer and the drum sounds (see pages 73–74). Like drum sounds, bass sounds vary from style to style. Some use an upright bass, others use one of the many different electric bass guitar voices (slap bass, picked bass, fingered bass...) or a synthesized bass sound, for example.

Acc1, acc2, acc3

The remaining tracks are dedicated to harmony and any additional instruments. They're usually marked acc1, acc2, acc3, and so on, acc being short for accompaniment.

Three to eight

The number of available tracks generally varies from three to eight. The more tracks you have, the more parts you can play simultaneously, and the more flexible your band is: You can usually choose which ones you want to hear and which ones you don't, or you can be accompanied by a drummer only, then add a bassist, then a pianist, a horn section, strings, a guitarist, backing vocalists... Advanced systems also allow you to set the volume level of each part or track.

Small and large

On some instruments, you can switch between small and large ensembles, or you have options for drum and bass, combo, or big band, for example. Also, you may be able to spice up the band with a series of buttons that activate a trumpet section, a steel drummer, a funky guitarist, or another musician that follows the chords you play. The choice of instrumentalists under these buttons is usually determined by the style you have chosen, but you may be allowed to make alternative selections.

Morphing

Some instruments allow for extra variations by letting you blend or morph parts from various styles. Samba drums and an upright bass in a hip hop band? No problem.

Lower

A button marked lower or left orchestra lets you add a voice to what you play with your left hand, so you can add strings to the band, or guitar chords, or any other sound.

Variations

All these possibilities add up to the pre-programmed style variations that every keyboard offers.

CHORD RECOGNITION

Keyboards and ensemble pianos have various chord

recognition modes. Here's what they are and how they work.

One finger

A popular function allows you to play chords with just a single finger. Some familiar names for this mode are *one-finger chords, single-finger chords,* or *intelligent chords.* In this mode, pressing a C key in the chord recognition area produces a C-major chord, sounding the notes C, E, and G. (For more information on chords, please check out *Tipbook Music on Paper,* see page 134.)

Keys are switches

To play a C-minor chord in this mode, sounding the notes C, E♭, and G, you need to press the C key and the white D key above it. Adding the next white key results in a C-major seven chord (C7), sounding the notes C, E, G, and B♭. In this mode, the keys become switches rather than keys: A single 'switch' produces a major chord, two adjacent switches produce a minor chord, and so on. This saves you from having to learn the way chords are built up. Some instruments can even produce minor, seventh, and other chords that match the key signature of the piece by pressing single keys only.

Fingered

In the fingered or fingered chords mode, you trigger the accompaniment by playing all the notes that make up the chord you want to hear.

Full keyboard

In a third mode (*piano style, whole key, full keyboard, full,* or *full range*), the entire keyboard is turned into a chord recognition area: The chords are deduced from the harmonies that you play, and you can play the melody or a solo simultaneously.

INTELLIGENT CHORDS

FINGERED CHORDS

FULL KEYBOARD

NORMAL

MODE

Normal

In the *normal* mode, the accompaniment section is deactivated. **Different modes.**

You may be able to keep a rhythmic backing going, but the rest of the band won't be around.

Bass inversion

Virtual bassists usually play the root note of the chord. A function with names such as *bass inversion* or *fingered-on bass* allows you to have your bassist play other notes as well: If you play a C-major chord as C-E-G, the bassist will play the root (C). If you invert the chord and play it as E-G-C, for example, you will hear an E instead.

G nine sharp eleven

There are many more chord types than the three mentioned above. All instruments will recognize the common chord types, and a growing number of accompaniment systems can also handle extended chords that include, for example, a ninth and a raised eleventh step (*e.g.*, C9♯11: C-E-G-B♭-D-F♯).

CONTROLING THE BAND

Songs always consist of various sections linked to one another in sequence. They often start off with an intro, followed by a number of verses and choruses, and then finish off with an ending. Accompaniment sections help you emulate a real band by offering one or more automatic intros and endings, variations on the basic pattern that you can use for the choruses, and fills to link the sections to one another. More money usually buys you more options and more flexibility.

Accompaniment controls (GEM).

Intros and endings

Playing an intro is usually a matter of providing the desired chord and hitting the intro button. To have the

instrument provide a fully automatic ending, you simply hit the ending button. Better instruments offer a choice of (shorter, longer, and so on) intros and endings.

Variations

You'll often use the basic pattern in a certain style for the verse of a song and select a variation for the chorus. These variations usually sound a bit busier than the basic pattern. A guitar riff may be spiced up, the drummer may switch from timekeeping on the hi-hat to the ride cymbal, horns may be added, the feel or the rhythm may be changed, and so on.

Synchro start and stop

When you use synchro start, the band won't kick in until you play a chord. This allows you to play an intro melody with your right hand, dropping the accompaniment in later with your left. Synchro stop stops the band when you release the keys in the chord recognition area.

Hold

The hold option, permanently switched on in most instruments, does the opposite of synchro stop: It ensures the band keeps playing whether you are playing or not. Switching hold off, if the instrument has that option, will stop the chord and bass parts of the accompaniment as soon as you release the keys – only the drums continue.

More than one

Advanced instruments offer a variety of endings, intros, variations, and fills or breaks per style. Some can automatically play a fill when you go from one variation to the next, others only when you tell them to.

Fade out, fade in

Some instruments have a fade out function, so you can gradually reduce the sound to silence rather than using an ending. Fade in does the opposite.

Mix 'n' match

Fully-featured auto-accompaniments allow you to mix and match all kinds of options: fills with variations, synchro starts with intros, and so on.

Groove control

Some keyboards also allow for groove control, slightly altering the exact timing of the band to create a different, more 'human' rhythmic feel.

Softer, please

You can usually adjust the balance between the accompaniment and the melody part you play, but you'll get a more musical performance if you can control the loudness of the band real time, by simply changing the velocity at which you play the chords: When you play softer, the band follows – just like a real ensemble would, or at least should – and vice versa.

DO-IT-YOURSELF

Sophisticated instruments often let you create your own styles or edit existing ones by changing bass patterns, adding instruments, changing voices, editing effects, reducing the percussion section, or whatever you like.

Save

You can always save the styles you've made or edited. You may able to save anywhere from eight up to 64 or more *user styles* or *RAM styles* next to the available, pre-programmed *ROM styles*. This is the maximum number of user styles that you can access directly; of course you can save more styles on disk, for example.

From scratch

Programming a full accompaniment from scratch is not easy: Every part and every section has to be composed and programmed into the sequencer.

8. CONNECTIONS

Headphones, amplifiers, additional instruments, mixers, you name it: Most keyboards and pianos come with a host of inputs and outputs for a host of possibilities.

Pedal connections (*control jacks*) have been covered in Chapter 5; MIDI connections are dealt with in Chapter 9. The other connections are explained in this chapter.

Before

Before you connect any cords to your instrument or any other electric or electronic devices, always read the relevant manuals. Also, turn all relevant volume controls all the way down when connecting or disconnecting musical instruments, amplifiers, and other devices, and be sure that all devices have their power turned off.

In and out

Connections are also known as (*connection*) *terminals*, *sockets*, *receptacles*, or *jacks*. Some are inputs, which feed data or electric signals (*i.e.*, power or audio signals) into the instrument. Other jacks are outputs, from where data or signals can be sent to other devices: mixers, speakers, an amplifier, or your computer, for example.

Where

With the exception of the headphone jack(s), the connections are usually located on the rear panel of the instrument. Some manufacturers identify these connections on the front panel to make it easier to plug in or remove cables from corresponding positions in the back. A few

instruments have their connections on the left side panel.

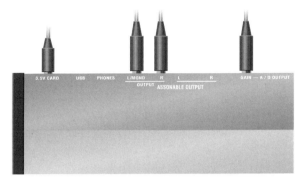

3.5V CARD   USB   PHONES   L/MONO   R   L   R   GAIN — A / D OUTPUT
OUTPUT   ASSONABLE OUTPUT

... identify the connections on the front panel...

Headphones

Most instruments have their headphone jack(s) below the keyboard, on the left-hand side. Having two headphone jacks is useful for lessons (one for you, one for your teacher), or if you want to play four-handed classical music on a digital piano, for example. Most headphone jacks are designed for 1/4" TRS phono plugs. TRS stands for tip, ring, and sleeve. Three wires can be attached to this plug (ground, left, and right), so it allows for the transmission of a stereo signal.

Audio out

The audio outputs, labeled *line out*, *audio out*, or just *output*, are used to connect the instrument to an external sound system, a mixer, or the line inputs of another

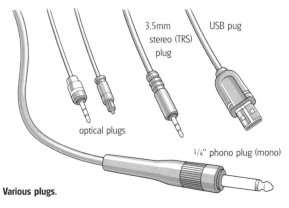

3.5mm
stereo (TRS)
plug

USB pug

optical plugs

1/4" phono plug (mono)

Various plugs.

instrument. There's usually one connector for the right channel and one for the left. One of them will be labeled mono, usually the left one ('L/MONO'). If you have a mono keyboard amp, use this socket. Audio outputs and inputs use large (1/4") phono plugs.

Prevent overload

If you don't have separate audio outputs and you still want to use external amplification, you may try to use the headphone jack instead. Note that this output produces a pretty strong signal. Set the volume control on your instrument no higher than a quarter of the way, and then use the amp's volume control as the master control. This will usually prevent overload and possible damage to the amp and speakers. Remember that a dedicated audio output is better suited to the task of driving an external amplifier, so if your instrument has one, use it.

Assignable outputs

Assignable outputs – very rare on the instruments covered in this book – let you send a particular track or a part of your performance to an external device. An example would be to use an external reverb, a distortion, or another effect on a certain part.

Multimedia speakers

Speaker-less stage pianos sometimes have a stereo mini-jack that you can use for a pair of multimedia monitor speakers so you can practice at low volumes.

Line in

The *line* or *audio in* connectors can be used to connect another instrument (so it uses the same amp and speakers as your instrument), or a CD player or another sound source, so that you can play along with the music. Line inputs can also be used for sampling purposes. Similar to the audio outputs, you need to use the one marked 'mono' if you want to connect a mono device.

Various connections.

Effects

The line input is usually not routed through the internal effects: If you connect another instrument to this input, its sound will not be affected by the effects section of the main instrument.

Gain control

Because different devices generate different output levels, it is helpful if the inputs have an adjustable *gain control* or *trim control*. This allows you to adjust the sensitivity of the input to match the connected equipment.

Anything

Some inputs can handle anything from another electronic instrument or a CD-player (high output) to an electric guitar (relatively low output) or a microphone (very low output).

Microphones

If your instrument has a dedicated microphone input, it will usually also have dedicated vocal effects too (see page 65) that affect the signal from this input only. Of course, you can also use the microphone input for an acoustic guitar or the sound of any other instrument. A gain control is usually provided. Check the manual to see which type of microphone is recommended.

Send and return

A few instruments have special inputs and outputs to connect an internal effect device. They are usually labeled *send* or *auxiliary output* and *loop return* or *auxiliary input* respectively. The output transmits the signal to the effect; the loop return receives the processed signal.

Digital in/out

Digital inputs and outputs (AES/EBU or S/PDIF) are occasionally found on keyboards and digital pianos. They're commonly used in studios only. Optical connectors use light to transmit data.

Video out

A *video output* allows you to connect a TV monitor to view karaoke style lyrics, or display a slide show to enhance your music.

COMPUTER CONNECTIONS

You can connect your instrument to your computer using MIDI (see Chapter 9), but some instruments have alternative connectors too.

To host

Some keyboard instruments have a direct computer connection, usually marked *to host* or simply *computer.* Depending on the software that is either supplied with the instrument or available as an option, you can now use your computer for a variety of purposes, from recording and playing back your performances to saving or loading sounds, styles, and other data, editing and printing the music you played, and so on.

USB port

If the instrument can be connected to a computer with a USB port, the computer will recognize it as an extra hard disk, allowing you to exchange data with the familiar drag and drop technique. You can make audio recordings of your performances and store them on your computer's hard disk, burn them onto CD-Rs, or convert them into smaller MP3 or WMF files and send them to friends over the Internet, and so on. On some instruments, the USB port is used for MIDI too (see page 100).

SCSI interface

With a *SCSI* interface, you can connect an external (*peripheral*) drive to your instrument, *i.e.*, a hard disk, which allows you to manage and save big quantities of data.

PC keyboard

A few instruments have an input for a computer keyboard, which you can use to enter lyric data into songs, or to give names to sounds, styles, or songs.

9. MIDI

Layering sounds is a great way to expand your creative possibilities. It's even better if you can layer the sounds of different instruments: Play one keyboard and have a voice of another keyboard or a synthesizer sound along. This is just one of the many possibilities offered by MIDI. This chapter tells you the basics.

MIDI is a system that allows electronic musical instruments to communicate with each other. The four letters stand for *Musical Instrument Digital*

The in and out ports of the built-in MIDI interface.

Interface: It allows a digital connection (interface) between musical instruments. Every digital keyboard instrument has special in and out ports to establish this connection.

Piano and strings

Suppose you have a digital piano and a portable keyboard, and you want to combine the grand piano voice of the

This way, you can add the sound of the keyboard to what you play on the piano.

piano with the keyboard's strings. You'll need to make the two instruments communicate with each other. How? You simply connect the MIDI Out port on the piano to the keyboard's MIDI In port. Then you select the sounds you want to use on each instrument, you play the piano, and you will hear the keyboard play along. That's all.

Master

In this setup, the piano is the *master instrument*. The master instrument controls the *slave instrument*, in this case the keyboard. When you play the key C4 on the piano, MIDI tells the keyboard to do the same: It sends out a *Note On* message for the key C4. In MIDI, this key has *note number* 60.

Velocity and Note Off

How hard you play the key is converted to a *Velocity message*, with a value that can vary from 1 (as softly as possible) to 127 (as loudly as possible). Thus, the keyboard will start sounding louder as you play louder, and vice versa. When you release the key, MIDI sends a *Note Off* message to the keyboard.

No sound

So MIDI is about messages or *events* – not about sound. All manufacturers use the same codes for the same events. These codes and many other agreements are defined in the *MIDI protocol*.

Control changes

The modulation wheel, for example, has been defined as controller #1: If you operate the modulation wheel on the master instrument, the slave instrument will respond accordingly. Likewise, you can use MIDI to send *control changes* to alter volume (controller #7), panorama or panning (#10), damper pedal (#64), effects, and so on. A *program change* is a command that instructs the slave instrument to use another sound.

Your computer

With MIDI, you can hook up your instrument to your computer too. For that purpose, your computer needs a sound card with a MIDI interface (usually recognizable

by two or more round, five-pin MIDI ports), or your instrument needs to have a USB port that doubles as a MIDI connection. Provided that you have the right software, you can now use your computer as a powerful sequencer, a recording studio, an interactive teacher, and much more, as you can read on pages 104–106.

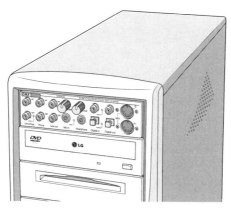

Front module of a MIDI-equipped sound card: MIDI in, MIDI out, and other connections (Terratec).

Warning
MIDI, again, is not sound. Never connect MIDI ports to an amplifier.

MULTIPLE INSTRUMENTS
With MIDI, you can connect multiple instruments simultaneously. Suppose you use your piano as the master instrument, and you want to hook up a keyboard for its beautiful strings, and a digital organ for its great tone wheel sound. To make sure that every instrument receives the right messages, MIDI uses 16 different *channels*. In this example, you would use channel 1 to send messages to the keyboard, and channel 2 for the organ. If you want to use different voices on one multitimbral keyboard, you have to assign each voice to a different channel.

One cable
All channels travel trough the same MIDI cable, just as all your TV channels use a single cable. You set the channel on each slave instrument, or for each voice, just like you

select a channel on your television: Setting a channel makes it respond to the information from that channel only.

Thru

In addition to MIDI in and out ports, many instruments have *MIDI thru.* You use this port if you want to connect multiple instruments. MIDI Thru transmits an exact copy of the information that was received at the MIDI in port.

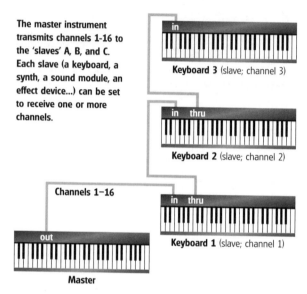

The master instrument transmits channels 1-16 to the 'slaves' A, B, and C. Each slave (a keyboard, a synth, a sound module, an effect device...) can be set to receive one or more channels.

Keyboard 3 (slave; channel 3)

Keyboard 2 (slave; channel 2)

Channels 1–16

Keyboard 1 (slave; channel 1)

Master

Daisy chaining

Connecting multiple instruments by using thru ports is known as *daisy-chaining.* If you daisy-chain more than four instruments or devices, the last device in the chain may not respond properly anymore: The chain has become too long.

MIDI Thru box

This can be solved with a *MIDI splitter* or *thru box* that has a single MIDI in and multiple MIDI out ports.

Dual ports

To prevent you from running short of channels, MIDI equipment sometimes comes with an extra set of MIDI ports. Dual ports provide you with double the number of MIDI channels.

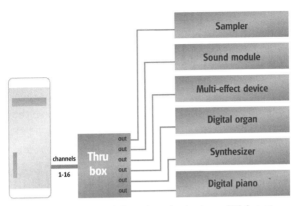

The computer transmits all channels to the thru box, which has an individual MIDI out for each device.

Studio

MIDI's multiple channels are often used in studios, where a single computer can be used to control numerous different instruments, sound modules, effects, or other devices. In live situations, MIDI can also be used to synchronize lighting cues with the music.

USB and MIDI

A growing number of instruments uses USB type ports for MIDI, in addition to the traditional five-pin MIDI ports. This has several advantages: The computer doesn't need to have a MIDI interface, you don't need special MIDI cables, and USB ports allow for faster data transmission. Traditional MIDI ports are still used for connections during live performances.

Music Local Area Network - mLAN

Yamaha has developed a new digital network for musical applications, called *mLAN*. This *music Local Area Network* uses a single firewire cable for all audio input and output and MIDI input and output, and it is capable of exchanging large files at high speed.

MIDI DEVICES

There are many different devices that have MIDI – from instruments to lighting equipment, effect devices, and so on. Here are some examples.

Sound modules

A sound module is basically an instrument without keys: You need MIDI to trigger its sound and effects. There are piano modules, organ modules, bass modules, synth modules, and so on. A sound module is a lot cheaper than the equivalent instrument with keys, of course.

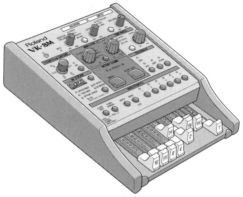

A organ rack module with various organ sounds, effects, drawbars (see pages 35-36) and related features. The same instrument is available with keys as well (Roland).

MIDI controllers

A *MIDI controller*, *master keyboard*, or *controller keyboard* is the reverse of a sound module, so to speak: These 'instruments' have no sounds or effects, but they output MIDI data to trigger sounds from other MIDI devices, such as sound modules or keyboard instruments. Apart from a keyboard, they feature pitch-bend and modulation wheels, and often a series of other real-time controllers, *e.g.*, a number of assignable rotary controls that can be

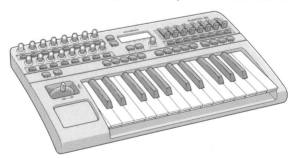

Affordable master keyboard with a two-octave keyboard, modulation, pitch bend, and a series of assignable rotary controllers (Novation).

used to set filters, effects, volume, and so on. Small (two- or three-octave) master keyboards have very friendly prices. When it comes to larger keyboards, an instrument with built-in sounds is usually preferred.

Multizone keyboards

Larger keyboard controllers often have various independent MIDI zones, which allows you to control as many MIDI devices with just one keyboard: Each zone can be assigned to a separate device or sound.

Other controllers

You don't need to be a keyboard player to use MIDI, as MIDI controllers come in other formats too, such as drum pads, MIDI guitars, or wind controllers.

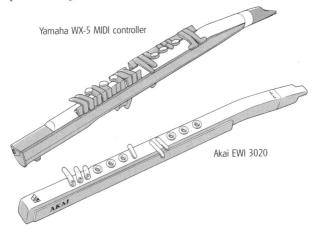

Yamaha WX-5 MIDI controller

Akai EWI 3020

These MIDI wind controllers were designed for saxophonists.

Hardware sequencers and samplers

MIDI can also be used in combination with dedicated devices such as hardware sequencers, samplers, or drum computers: big boxes that do just what their names suggest. Their popularity is decreasing as software-based versions increasingly take over their functions.

YOUR COMPUTER

Software can turn your computer into a sequencer, an interactive teacher, a sampler, and much more. You will

need dedicated software for most applications. This may be included with your sound card or your instrument. Professional level software usually needs to be bought separately.

Sequencers

The most popular musical application for computers is to use them as a sequencer. You can record your performance in as many steps as you have tracks available, and then edit the music, adding effects, correcting mistakes, changing the tempo, assigning other voices, and so on. With the computer's MIDI out connected to your keyboard's MIDI in, you can play back what you have created. (Most sound cards can play back the file too, but their built-in sound engines usually don't sound that good.)

Audio too

Most sequencer software doubles as a multitrack audio recorder, which turns your computer into a real digital recording studio. You can also add audio recordings (vocals, guitars, and so on) to your MIDI recordings and mix everything down to a final product that you can burn onto an audio CD-R.

Sampling

Computers can also be used as samplers: You can record the sound on your hard disk and play it back with your keyboard, or you can buy sample CDs or download samples from the Internet.

Transcriptions

Computers can be used to make real-time transcriptions of your performances. You can edit the transcription and have your computer play it back. The same software can usually be used to write music too: You put the notes on the staff with your (computer) keyboard or your mouse, and you can hear what your composition sounds like right away.

Interactive teacher

You can use your computer as an interactive teacher. There's educational software for almost any subject, from ear training to keyboard dexterity and advanced subjects such as counterpoint.

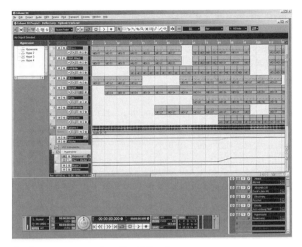

A software sequencer in action (Cubase).

Virtual pianos and keyboards

Similar to software sequencers and samplers, there are
software pianos, organs, and synthesizers too. You play these
virtual instruments with a keyboard that's connected to
your computer. They're a lot cheaper than the real thing,
as production costs are basically limited to copying CDs
and printing manuals.

GENERAL MIDI

Most keyboard instruments bear a logo with the words
General MIDI. This is a subset of agreements. One of the
General MIDI or *GM* agreements is that certain voices can
always be found on specified locations in the instrument's
memory. If you record a song on a GM instrument, this
means that this MIDI file will trigger the exact same voices
if you play it back on another GM instrument: It won't
sound a saxophone when it should have been a trumpet.

These logos show that the instrument is GM or GM2 compatible.

Agreements

Instruments with the General MIDI logo have at least 128
different voices in specified locations; they are at least

16-part multitimbral and they have at least 24-note polyphony. Another agreement is that MIDI channel 10 is always used for drum parts.

Level 2

GM dates back to 1991, eight years after MIDI was launched. A lot has happened since. The required number of 128 sounds, for instance, is now considered pretty low. It wasn't until 1999 that a new standard was set. This new standard, *General MIDI level 2* or *GM2*, extended the number of sounds to 256. It requires 32-note polyphony, and a lot of expressive musical parameters have been added. Some of these *continuous controllers* are reverb time, chorus rate, chorus depth, and fine tuning. GM2 devices are fully backward compatible with older standard MIDI files.

Proprietary formats

Quite a few manufacturers have introduced their own GM extensions. Roland has GS, Yamaha has XG and XF, GEM has GMX, and Technics has NX, for example. These formats usually have a lot more to offer than GM or GM2, but they're not mutually compatible. However, instruments with GS or other proprietary formats can commonly play back GM files. If you play back a file that was saved as one of these extended formats on a GM instrument, you will miss some of the extra features, which range from sounds to effects and variations.

10. MAINTENANCE

Electronic instruments require barely any maintenance, but treating them well may buy you reliability and a longer life expectancy.

Electronic instruments usually have something like 'Caution, risk of electric shock' written on their housing, as well as 'Do not open – no user serviceable parts inside.' Please take these and similar messages seriously. Apart from running the risk of personal injury, tampering with an instrument will almost certainly void the guarantee.

User's manual

Every user's manual includes a long list of things you should or shouldn't do. Please follow these guidelines carefully. And remember that this chapter doesn't replace or supersede your manual's safety instructions.

Stands

A special keyboard stand is a worthwhile investment for portable instruments. If you plan to take your instrument on the road, find one of the many designs that collapse into a flat pack for transport. A very common and easily adjustable design is the X-shaped stand, but there are other types too. Some offer finer height adjustment; others fold up more easily or weigh less, for example. If you want to alternate between standing up and sitting down as you play, the stand should accommodate both positions. Prices usually vary from about fifty to two hundred dollars. Some portable keyboard instruments have a matching stand as an option.

This easily adjustable stand collapses into a flat pack.

Expandable stand

If you plan to use more than one instrument simultaneously, get an expandable stand that can hold two or even three instruments. Check how easily it folds up with the expansion arms attached.

Shelf-mounted

If you play only at home, you can use a wall-mounted shelf instead. As a guide to height, the white keys of an acoustic piano are some 26" to 28" (66-72 cm) from the floor.

Moisture

Don't put drinks, flowers, or plants on your keyboard or pianos. Electronic instrument don't mix with liquids.

Hot and cold

Instruments never appreciate rapid temperature changes or extreme heat, cold, and humidity conditions. Keep your instrument away from direct sunlight, air conditioners, heating vents, fireplaces, and the like. Also be aware of the instrument's own cooling requirements, if it has any.

Display

If it does get very warm or cold, the display may become hard to read. It should return to normal when the temperature gets less extreme.

Static charge

Static charges can make your hair stand on end, or make sparks fly between yourself and a door handle. They can also damage electronic instruments. Apart from switching equipment on and off spontaneously, they may destroy delicate electronic components. Dry room conditions due to central heating or air conditioning often aggravate the build-up of static charges. Using a humidifier may help – and you may even try wearing shoes with leather soles.

Radio and TV

If you use the instrument too close to a TV or a radio, it may cause interference. If so, simply move one away from the other.

Cords

Always route cables so that they cannot be walked on or tripped over, and prevent them from being pinched by other instruments or objects. When gigging use *duct tape* (a.k.a. *stage tape* or *gaffer tape*) to fix cables to the floor.

Mains and adaptors

Disconnect the instrument from the mains if you're not going to be using it for a while. Most instruments leave their adaptors powered up when they're plugged in, and this wastes electricity. Be sure to use the correct power supply for your instrument. A 12-volt adaptor may seem to work on a 9-volt instrument, but the excessive voltage may shorten its working life.

Dust

Traditionally styled digital pianos often have a traditional key cover (the fallboard or *fall*) or a sliding key cover that protects the instrument from dust, airborne pollution, and so on. Instruments that don't can always be fitted with a removable protective cover, usually available for less than twenty dollars. Some covers have an adjustable cord for a snug fit.

Key cleaning

Keys can be carefully cleaned with the brush attachment on your vacuum cleaner. You can also use a clean, lint-free cloth. Always move from the back to the front of the keys

rather than sideways. If you use a cloth, you may moisten it with a mild soap solution or some glass cleaner. Never spray any type of cleaner onto the keys. The instrument's housing can be cleaned the same way – as long as you prevent anything beneath the keys and controls from getting wet. Also check the instrument's manual for specific information. Real wood cabinets require special care, as you can read in *Tipbook Piano*.

Nooks and crannies

You can use a fresh paintbrush to flick the dust from nooks and crannies. Avoid compressed-air spray cans; they just blow dust further into the instrument.

ON THE ROAD

When on the road, a *gig bag* helps to protect your instrument from minor knocks and scratches, and it makes it easier to carry. The bag should be water resistant and have solid grip handles. A shoulder strap can be very helpful. The zip should be smooth and strong. Gig bags often have one or more external zipper compartments for cables, pedals, switches, sheet music, and other accessories. Velcro fasteners inside prevent the instrument from falling out once you open the zipper. Damage of the outer skin is reduced if the bag has small rubber or metal feet, as well as corner and edge protectors. If you have a heavy instrument, consider getting a bag with wheels.

A gig bag with external compartments, corner protectors, Velcro fasteners inside, a shoulder strap...

More

Gig bag prices start around forty dollars. More money usually buys you better quality materials, heavier padding, and better zippers, among other things. Professional quality bags may cost up to two hundred.

Flight cases

Hard-shell cases generally offer more protection than gig-bags, but they're not as easy to carry around. And size is a critical issue: The fit for keyboard instruments into hard cases should be perfect. Some models feature adjustable sizing blocks. For serious gigging and touring you'll need a genuine *flight case*, which can be custom made. Flight cases are heavy and expensive, with prices going up to four hundred dollars and more.

Cords, backups, and insurance

- Always bring **spare cables** on the road – at least one of every type you use.
- Bring a **backup** of every floppy disk you use. Also keep backups at home: Should you lose all your gear, you won't have lost all your music.
- Consider **insuring your instrument**, especially if you're taking it on the road – which includes visiting your teacher. Musical instruments fall under the 'valuables' insurance category. A regular homeowner insurance policy will not cover all possible damage, whether it occurs at home, on the road, in the studio, or onstage.

11. BACK IN TIME

This chapter briefly traces the digital piano back to its acoustic ancestor, and the home keyboard back to the organ.

One of the earliest keyboard instruments is the *clavichord*, which was designed in the fourteenth century. *Clavis* means key; the *chords* were the instrument's strings. The working principles of the clavichord were later applied to the spinet and harpsichord: When a key is pressed, a small pick (a raven quill, actually) plucks the appropriate string.

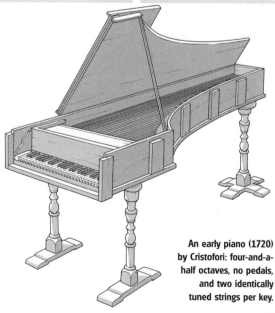

An early piano (1720) by Cristofori: four-and-a-half octaves, no pedals, and two identically tuned strings per key.

Pianofortes

The main drawback of these early instruments was their lack of touch sensitivity: Every note sounded equally loud. Around 1700, the Italian harpsichord maker Bartolomeo Cristofori began building an instrument that would bypass that limitation. He replaced the picks with hammers, which allowed the player to play softly (*piano*, in Italian) as well as loudly (*forte*). The obvious name for this new instrument, *pianoforte*, was later shortened to piano. Some twenty-five years after its introduction, Cristofori designed a new action, which was very similar to the present system.

Electric pianos

In the late 1940s the first electric pianos appeared, employing short strings, metal reeds, tines, or tone bars instead of full-length strings. The vibrations were converted to electrical signals by one or more pickups, similar to the ones found on electric guitars, and then sent to an amplifier.

Famous names   Tipcode KEYS-018

The production of *electric pianos* ceased in the late 1970s and early 1980s. They're still heard today, however – as either the original instruments themselves or sampled versions that can be found in most keyboards and digital pianos. The Fender Rhodes is probably the most popular example. To avoid copyright problems, Rhodes-samples

Fender Rhodes Stage Piano.

are often dubbed Rhodex or simply EP (electric piano), for example. The sampled sounds vary a great deal, as the original instrument can be adjusted to produce a wide range of related, yet distinctly different timbres. Another popular sound is that of the Wurlitzer electric piano, used in hit albums such as Supertramp's *Crime of the Century*. Hohner's Clavinet used short strings and guitar pickups. Designed as an electric alternative to the harpsichord, it became extremely popular in funk and rock bands. A famous song with a prominent role for the Clavinet is Stevie Wonder's *Superstition*.

Electric grand

Another classic sound, Yamaha's electric grand pianos, was introduced in the late 1970s and can now be found in the collection of many keyboards and digital pianos. The electric grand had short, real piano strings, and it sounded, just as its name suggests, like an electric grand piano.

Digital pianos

In 1983, Yamaha introduced the first digital piano, and Kurzweil presented the first digital sampling keyboard.

KEYBOARDS

The keyboard evolved from the organ, and the organ itself is a distant descendant of the panpipes: a row of cane tubes, each of which is tuned to a specific pitch, played the same way as you would 'play' a bottle by blowing into it. A traditional organ is basically a mechanical set of panpipes. The air stream is produced by a bellows and controlled from the keyboard. The effect of using pipes or *flutes* of different lengths to produce various timbres was later emulated by the Hammond organ's drawbars (see pages 35–36).

Upper and lower

Organs often have two keyboards or *manuals*, as shown in the illustration on page 117. The terms *lower manual* and *upper manual* for the left- and right-hand section of a modern keyboard stem from these dual-manual organs.

Electronic organ

The first electronic organs date from the 1940s. Most of

them used vacuum tubes like those found in tube amplifiers and old radios. Just like tube radios, the original tube organs were eventually replaced by transistorized *solid state* models. During the 1960s and 1970s, the electronic organ played a leading role on the keyboard market.

One finger

The 1970s saw the arrival of the first electronic organs with primitive drum machines built in. Full accompaniment sections soon followed. A Dutch company named Riha pioneered a system that allowed entire orchestrations to be played with just one finger.

Analog to digital

The first electronic organs used analog technology. Filters were applied to shape the vibrations into a wide variety of sounds, including simulations of certain instruments. Then, just as pianos went digital, so did organs. At that point, electronic organs could sound like any instrument: The (home or portable) keyboard was born.

Synthesizers

The first really useful synthesizers were made in the 1960s. The most famous vintage synth is the Minimoog (1972–1980), a monophonic analog instrument that is still very popular – so popular, in fact, that a new version was introduced in 2002. Other companies make digital synths that emulate the 'fat' sounds of their analog predecessors of the 1970s.

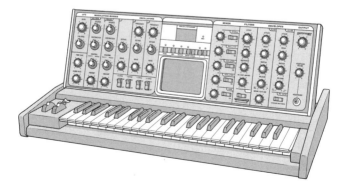

The 2002 Minimoog Voyager.

TONE WHEEL ORGANS

Patented by Hammond in 1934, the Hammond tone wheel organ has a notched, rotating 2″ disc for each note and a magnetic pickup for each disc. The notches produce changes in the magnetic field of the pickups, similar to what the vibrating strings of an electric guitar do. The number of notches (two for the lowest note, 256 for the highest note) determines the pitch.

B-3

Tipcode KEYS-019

The B-3, Hammond's best-known model, was made from 1954 to 1974. Even though it has been digitally emulated, with designs that duplicate the original instrument at a fraction of its 400-pound weight, the vintage B-3 is still preferred over these newer models by many rock and jazz musicians.

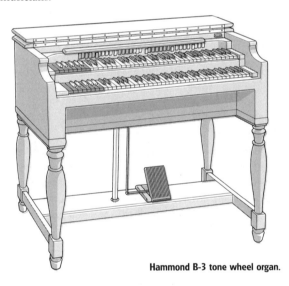

Hammond B-3 tone wheel organ.

Leslie

The Hammond B-3 is hardly complete without a Leslie speaker cabinet, which has a rotating horn for the treble range and a rotating drum that swirls and projects the frequencies produced by the woofer. Since Leslie is a registered trademark, digital simulations of this effect are given alternative names such as *rotor*, *rotary*, or *spatial sound*.

12. THE FAMILY

Some of the instruments from the previous chapter still are and will always be living members of the keyboard family. This chapter introduces some of their younger relatives.

Digital keyboard instruments can be hard to categorize. That goes for keyboards and digital pianos (and the combination of the two, the ensemble piano) as well as for synthesizers, workstations, and samplers, as you will see below.

Synthesizers

Rather than just offer a number of preset voices, a typical synthesizer allows you to create (*synthesize*) completely original sounds. Providing you with raw samples or electronically generated tones and a wide range of filters (see page 66), a synth has all the tools you need to mold sounds into almost any shape you like.

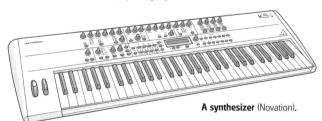

A synthesizer (Novation).

Sample players

Other synthesizers are mainly designed to emulate existing sounds. The main differences between these instruments

(sometimes labeled *sample players*) and keyboards are that these synths have more sound editing capabilities.

Workstations

A *workstation* is a self-contained compositional tool that commonly houses a complete set of samples, a powerful multitrack sequencer, a large effects section, a disk drive, one or more arpeggiators, and much more. Some workstations are based on a synthesizer platform; others are closer to a home keyboard, providing you with fully editable orchestras. Many of them are GM or GM2 compatible. Workstations were originally designed to create music from scratch, but instruments that are meant for live work are sometimes labeled (arranger) workstations too.

Samplers

Synths and workstations can have a built-in sampler, but there are dedicated hardware samplers too, either with or without a keyboard. Samplers usually have sound editing facilities similar to those on synths.

All in one

A growing number of instruments combines various features in one machine, resulting in *music production synthesizers, sampling workstations, synthesizer workstations, workstation keyboards,* and so on.

Groove machine

Another type of keyboard instrument is commonly known as *groove machine.* You can play it like a regular keyboard, but you can also use the keys as buttons that trigger preset or programmable DJ-oriented phrases, patterns, sounds, and effects, or to vary the voices that sound in a pattern so you can build it up instrument by instrument, for example. Special controllers allow you to emulate scratches or to change the pitch of a pattern without affecting the tempo, and more.

Remote keyboards

A *remote keyboard* allows you to move around like a guitarist or a bass player, with the instrument slung around your neck. The keyboard remotely controls a MIDI sound source.

CHAPTER 12

45-key remote keyboard (Roland).

Hybrid piano

A *hybrid piano* is an acoustic piano with a (MIDI) sound module that works just like on a digital piano: The movement of the keys and pedals are registered by sensors that are connected to the sound module. To use the digital sounds only, you lower a mute rail that stops the hammers before they hit the strings. Beside piano samples and other voices, sound modules may also provide you with accompaniments, a CD-player or CD-burner, and various other features.

Organs

Today's electronic organs and home keyboards are very similarly equipped, with a few exceptions: Organs have more organ sounds, they always come with bass pedals (see page 38), and they have a volume pedal and twin keyboards – essential features for lots of organ music.

Accordions

The *accordion* is a keyboard instrument too. The left hand usually uses small, round buttons to control a combination of bass notes and chords. The right hand, playing the melody, has either a standard keyboard layout or a button keyboard, also known as chromatic keyboards. Accordions can be fitted with MIDI.

Accordion keyboards

Accordion keyboards look like a portable keyboard instrument, but they have two separate manuals: a chromatic one for the left hand, and either a chromatic keyboard or a regular keyboard for the right hand.

13. BRANDS

The companies in the first section of this chapter all produce a relatively wide range of keyboards and digital pianos. The companies in the second section are either smaller or have a more specialized catalog in this field.

Please note that companies can suddenly disappear, expand, or change their production, so some of the information below may be outdated by the time you read it.

CASIO Since scoring a massive hit by introducing the world's first home keyboard, the VL-Tone, in 1981, Casio has focused on the lower and low-mid price ranges in its keyboard line. The company also makes digital pianos and a host of other electronic products, from cameras to cash registers.

Casio VL-Tone: a miniature keyboard with
ten rhythms, five sounds, and
a calculator.

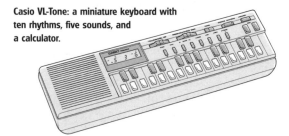

GEM by GENERALMUSIC Generalmusic is Italy's largest maker of keyboards and digital pianos, with an emphasis on mid- and pro-level instruments. The company premiered the multimedia keyboard as well as physical modeling for digital pianos.

CHAPTER 13

KORG Korg began life in the 1970s as a synthesizer manufacturer. The Japanese company makes arranger keyboards and digital pianos in the mid and high price ranges, along with workstations (their specialty), synths, samplers, and related equipment.

Roland® Founded in Japan in 1972, Roland soon grew to be one of the world's largest manufacturers of electronic musical instruments. It offers a huge choice of musical products, including all sorts of keyboard instruments, effects (under the Roland and Boss names), amplifiers, sequencers, electronic drum sets, and so on.

Technics Technics (Japan), originally known for their hi-fi equipment, makes low-budget, intermediate, and professional keyboards and pianos under the Technics and Panasonic brand names, as well as cameras, home appliances, and other electronic products.

YAMAHA® Yamaha started as a one-man organ factory in 1889. Besides electronic instruments and home electronics, the Japanese company produces acoustic instruments (pianos, drums, guitars, brasswinds, woodwinds, and so on) as well as sailing boats, motorcycles, and much more. All products show the company's musical heritage: the logo with the three tuning forks.

OTHER BRANDS

The companies in the following section are smaller, often more specialized players in the keyboard and digital piano market.

Digital pianos

Kawai (Japan), well known for its acoustic pianos and grands, debuted in the field of electronics in the late 1980s. The company makes digital pianos in all price ranges. Another company that markets both acoustic and digital pianos is **Weber**, founded by a German piano maker who

came to the US in 1844. **Kurzweil** started out as a US company producing high quality synthesizers. They also make upmarket digital pianos and grands for home and stage use. **Suzuki**, from Japan, makes the word's largest digital grand piano, a 5'9" model. Their digital pianos span all price ranges.

Italy

Due to its accordion and organ making tradition, Italy has a relatively large number of keyboard and digital piano manufacturers: Generalmusic (mentioned above), **Orla**, **Ketron**, and **Viscount**. **Farfisa** is another Italian name; their organs were very popular in 1960s and 1970s rock bands. The catalogs of both Orla and Viscount include organs and other instruments and sound equipment, along with their pianos and keyboards. Ketron used to be known as Solton; this company focuses on digital pianos and modules.

And more

In Germany, organ maker **Wersi** debuted the first keyboard with a full-blown Windows PC inside. Other brands that you may come across are **Madison**, **Medelli**, and **Valdesta**. **Post Musical Instruments** is a small Dutch company that produces pianos with over 5GB of samples for the grand piano voice.

Discontinued

Some companies that used to market digital pianos for a period of time are **Baldwin** (longtime US maker of acoustic pianos; marketed Pianovelle digital pianos), **Daewoo** (from Korea), **Alesis** (US company, well known for their studio equipment and effects), and **Ensoniq** (US company; now E-mu).

GLOSSARY AND INDEX

This glossary briefly explains most of the terminology touched on so far. The numbers refer to the page(s) where each term is covered in more detail. Proprietary terms are not included; please refer to the relevant manufacturer's website for information on their meaning.

Acc. See: *Auto accompaniments.*

Acoustic piano *(6, 13, 22–23, 28–30, 114, 120)* Predecessor of the digital piano. Has a wooden housing and soundboard, 88 keys, and about 220 plain and wound strings, which are struck by felt-tipped wooden hammers.

Action *(6, 8, 28–30, 114)* The mechanism that you operate by depressing the keys. Very important in how the instrument feels to play. Digital pianos usually have *weighted* or *hammer(ed) action keys*, which emulate the feel of an acoustic piano. Keyboards have *non-weighted, synth-action keys*.

Adaptor *(110)* Transformer; external power supply.

ADSR *(66)* Short for attack, decay, sustain, and release. These four parameters make up the *envelope* of the sound: the way in which it builds up and tails off. Also known as *envelope generator.*

Aftertouch *(31)* Allows you to manipulate the sound by pushing the key(s) down a little further after you've depressed them.

AIFF file *(59)* Macintosh format for audio files.

Amplification *(11, 40, 80–84)* The built-in or external amplifier and speakers.

Arpeggiator *(63)* Arpeggio means 'broken chord.' An arpeggiator generates sequences of separate notes triggered by the chord or the notes you play.

Assignable *(32, 38, 95, 103)* Some connections, controls, and pads can be assigned various functions.

Attack See: *ADSR.*

Auto(matic) accompaniments *(2–3, 8–9, 85–92)* Automatic virtual backing bands or orchestras, usually consisting of a rhythm section (drums, bass) and other instruments (acc 1, acc 2, and so on). Also labeled *accompany, arranger, rhythm, conductor,* or *style.*

Balance *(48, 49–50, 92)* Control used to set the relative levels of layered sounds, splits, the various parts of the accompaniment, or the left and right loudspeakers.

Bass pedal *(38)* Foot-operated keyboard.

Bit depth *(60)* Important figure in determining the quality of samples.

BPM *(41)* The tempo of a piece of music is expressed in BPM: beats per minute.

Break See: *Fill.*

CC *(107)* Used to indicate *continuous controller* or *control change,* both of which refer to MIDI messages that are used to control parameters such as volume and effect settings.

Channel 1. *(100–102)* MIDI uses sixteen channels; this allows you to independently control sixteen different instruments or timbres. **2.** *(81)* Stereo uses two channels.

Chord *(8, 16, 88–90)* Three or more simultaneously sounding notes make up a chord. Home keyboards offer a variety of systems that 'deduce' the right chord from your playing, using one, two, or more keys.

Chorus See: *Effects.*

Control jack *(93)* Jack input for a controller, *e.g.,* a volume pedal.

Data entry wheel *(46)* Rotary dial used to change a variety of settings. Also known as *alpha dial, jog wheel,* or simply *dial.*

Delay 1. *(61)* See: *Effects.* **2.** *(64)* Effect parameter.

Disk drive *(13, 58, 67)* An

onboard or external (floppy or hard) disk drive allows you to store or load songs, sounds, and other data.

Display *(10, 11, 41–43)* Pianos often have small numeric displays, while those on keyboards are big enough to show the selected sounds, keys, effects, and more.

Drawbars *(35–36)* Controls that add specific overtones to the (organ) sound you play.

DSP *(61)* Digital Signal Processor. Generates and controls sound effects. See: *Effects*.

Dual mode, dual voice See: *Layer*.

Dynamics, dynamic range *(31, 77, 81)* An instrument has good dynamics if it can play very softly, very loudly, and everywhere in between.

Editing *(57, 60, 65, 92)* Altering sounds or MIDI files, for example.

Effects *(12, 33, 51, 60–65)* Sound enhancers. Popular effects include reverb and delay (ambient effects), chorus, phasing, and flanging (modulation effects).

Electric piano *(114–115)* Predecessor of the digital piano.

Ensemble piano *(9, 118)* Semi-generic name for digital piano with accompaniments and other features. Also known as *intelligent piano* or *rhythm piano*.

Envelope, envelope generator See: *ADSR*.

Equalizer, EQ *(50–51)* Tone control, allowing you to alter the timbre of the sound by boosting or cutting bass, mid, and treble or even more frequency ranges.

Event *(55, 99)* A (MIDI) sequencer records events, not sounds. A key going down is one event, the velocity of the key is another, and so is the release of the key.

Expression pedal See: *Pedals*.

Fader *(32–33)* A sliding control as opposed to a rotary control.

FDD Floppy disk drive. See: *Disk drive*.

Fill *(9)* Short (rhythmical) variation, usually applied when going from one

song section to the other. Sometimes dubbed *break* – though a break more commonly means a few counts of silence in a piece.

Filter *(66, 116)* One of the main parts of a synthesizer's processing capabilities, used to shape sound. A low pass filter, for example, is used to control the amount of high frequencies in a sound by letting the low ones pass unaffected.

Floppy disk drive See: *Disk drive.*

General MIDI (GM) *(58, 106–107)* Addition to the original MIDI standard, containing specific assignments of sound numbers, channels, and more. See also: *MIDI.*

GM See: *General MIDI.*

Grand piano *(46)* Acoustic piano with a horizontal (as opposed to vertical) soundboard and strings.

Hammer(ed) action See: *Action.*

Hammond organ *(35, 117)* Electric organ with spinning tone wheels.

Hybrid piano *(120)* Acoustic piano with a

built-in sound module.

Jack *(93)* Connector.

Key shapes *(28)* Keyboard instruments can have *waterfall keys*, *piano-style/box-type keys*, or *overhanging/synth-type keys*.

Keyboard A word with many meanings. First and foremost, it is used to designate the common controller of all keyboard instruments, also known as the *manual*. Secondly, it is used to indicate the type of electronic keyboard musical instrument that has an auto accompaniment system. Thirdly, it may indicate any or all instruments that have a keyboard – from grand pianos to synthesizers.

Layer *(12, 48–49)* The *layer* feature allows you to stack two or more sounds on top of each other. Also known as *dual mode* or *dual voice.*

Lower, lower manual *(12, 47, 115)* Indicates the left side of the keyboard; upper indicates the right side. Stems from organs that have two keyboards, an upper one a lower one. See also: *Split.*

Manual 1. *(44)* Virtually

indispensable handbook for most keyboard instruments. **2.** *(5, 47)* Another word for the keyboard of an instrument.

Master instrument *(99, 101)* The instrument that you use to control other instruments or devices.

Memory *(6, 55, 57, 59, 75–76)* All data (*e.g.*, sounds, styles, the operating system) are stored in digital memory. There are two basic types of memory: ROM and RAM. Data in RAM (Random Access Memory) can be edited. Data in ROM (Read Only Memory) can't.

Metronome *(10, 11)* A device that emits beeps or clicks to state the tempo. Usually built-in.

MIDI *(15, 98–107)* Short for Musical Instrument Digital Interface. Allows digital instruments and other equipment to communicate with each other.

MIDI file See: *Standard MIDI file.*

MIDI in, MIDI out, MIDI thru *(98–99, 101)* Connections for receiving, transmitting, and retransmitting MIDI information.

Modulation 1. *(12–13, 33–34)* A *modulation wheel* is a control commonly used to make the sound vibrate (a slight rapid alternation of the pitch). **2.** *(61)* Chorus, flanger, and phaser are commonly known as modulation effects.

Multimedia keyboard *(43)* Home keyboard with TV and/or monitor connections.

Multitimbral *(53, 54)* A multitimbral instrument is able to produce several different sounds at the same time. Most keyboards are 16-part multitimbral.

Multitrack See: *Track.*

Note number *(99)* For MIDI purposes, every pitch has a note number assigned to it.

Octave *(5, 27)* Twelve consecutive white and black keys make up an octave. The size of a keyboard is often expressed as the number of octaves it covers.

Organ *(37, 115–117)* The predecessor of the home keyboard.

Pad sounds *(73)* Special type of synthetic sounds,

often used for backgrounds.

Pedals *(13–14, 36–38)* Pedals can be used for a variety of functions. Typical uses include to sustain (*damper*), control volume, start and stop the accompaniments, and so on. An expression pedal *(*)* usually controls volume.

Pitch bend *(12–13, 33–34)* A feature allowing you to bend the pitch of the notes up or down, usually controlled by a wheel or a joystick.

Polyphonic *(31, 53–54)* A 24-voice polyphonic instrument is capable of sounding 24 notes (voices) simultaneously. Early synthesizers were monophonic: They produced a single note at a time.

Preset *(61, 118)* A preset sound is pre-programmed by the manufacturer of the instrument. User presets can be modified by the user.

Quantizing *(56)* Sequencers record events in 'steps,' distributing the notes in a timing grid. The finer this grid, the higher the quantize resolution (expressed in ppq: pulses per quarter note), and

the more accurate the recording. A low quantize resolution can be used to solve timing problems when recording. See also: *Resolution.*

RAM See: *Memory.*

Real-time controller *(34–35)* Allows you to change volume, effect settings, and other elements in real time, *i.e.*, while you're playing.

Release velocity *(31–32)* Lets you control the sound by how fast you let the keys return to their original position.

Resolution *(56)* The higher the resolution, the better the sequencer records timing subtleties. Thrown in a wheelbarrow, a load of bricks will roughly take on the shape of the barrow. A load of sand will do so far more accurately. In other words, sand has a higher 'resolution' than bricks.

Reverb See: *Effects.*

Ribbon controller *(34)* Controller operated by sliding a finger over it.

ROM See: *Memory.*

Sample *(6, 60, 74–76)* Digitally recorded sound.

Sampler *(59–60)* A device to record, manipulate, and play back samples. See also: *Sample*.

Sampling rate *(60)* Important figure in determining the quality of samples.

Sequencer *(10, 13, 54–57, 104, 105–106)* Digital recorder of electronic musical events, as opposed to a recorder of sounds. Keyboard instruments usually have one on board.

SMF See: *Standard MIDI File*.

Soft keys *(33, 45)* Control buttons on the perimeter of a display, used to select items from information in the display. As the information changes, so do the functions of the buttons.

Sound module *(103, 120)* You can expand your instrument with sound modules, which offer additional sounds and other features.

Split *(10, 12, 47–48)* Allows you to use different sounds on the left (lower) and right (upper) side of the keyboard.

Stage piano *(7, 39, 114)*

Digital piano designed for onstage use. Usually lacks built-in speakers.

Stand *(108–109)* Most keyboard stands have an X-shaped design.

Standard MIDI File (SMF) *(57–59)* Most sequencers can read and save Standard MIDI files. Standard MIDI files can have various formats, *e.g.*, General MIDI, XS, and GX.

Synthesizer *(13, 65–66, 116, 118–119)* Electronic musical instrument designed to create, program, manipulate, and play sounds.

Touch sensitivity *(6, 30, 49)* An instrument with a touch sensitive keyboard sounds louder the harder you strike the keys, and vice versa. Also referred to as *touch response* and *velocity sensitivity*.

Track 1. *(87–88)* Each part of an accompaniment is assigned to a separate track. **2.** *(56)* Most sequencers have multiple tracks to allow several parts to be recorded independently of each other and played back simultaneously (*multi-tracking*).

Transpose *(10, 49, 53)* By

transposing an instrument's pitch, you can make it sound higher or lower (in half tone steps, up to one or more octaves).

Tuning *(51–52)* Most instruments can have their overall pitch finely adjusted up or down a small amount. Some digital pianos can be tuned one key at a time.

Upper, upper manual See: *Lower, lower manual.*

Velocity See: *Touch sensitive.*

Vibrato See: *Modulation.*

Waterfall keys See: *Key shapes.*

WAV-file *(59)* Common format to save audio files.

Weighted keyboard See: *Action.*

Workstation *(119)* Electronic musical instrument that commonly houses samples, a sequencer, effects, a disk drive, an arpeggiator, and many other features.

TIPCODE LIST

The Tipcodes in this book offer easy access to short movies, photo series, soundtracks, and other additional information at www.tipbook.com. For your convenience, the Tipcodes in this Tipbook have been listed below.

Tipcode	Topic	Page	Chapter
KEYS-001	The C, the F, and the octave	5	2
KEYS-002	Some voices of a digital piano	7	2
KEYS-003	Intros and endings	9	2
KEYS-004	Variations and fills	9	2
KEYS-005	Layers	12	2
KEYS-006	Pitch bend and modulation	12	2
KEYS-007	Draw bars	35	5
KEYS-008	One key, various sounds	47	5
KEYS-009	Fine tuning	51	5
KEYS-010	Reverb, chorus, and other effects	60–62	5
KEYS-011	Harmony types	63	5
KEYS-012	Arpeggiator	63	5
KEYS-013	Depth, rate, and level	63	5
KEYS-014	Envelope generator	66	5
KEYS-015	Filters	66	5
KEYS-016	Synthesizer and pad sounds	73	6
KEYS-017	An octave higher	74	6
KEYS-018	Electric pianos	114	11
KEYS-019	Hammond B3	117	11

WANT TO KNOW MORE?

Tipbooks supply you with basic information on the instrument of your choice and everything that comes with it. Of course, there's a lot more to be found on all subjects you came across on these pages.*

MAGAZINES

Reviews of keyboards, digital pianos, and related equipment can be found in many general music magazines. A few specialized US magazines also feature articles and news on other electronic instruments and devices.

- *Keyboard*, phone (800) 289-9919 or (850) 682-7644, www.keyboardmag.com or www.keyboardonline.com
- *Electronic Musician*, phone (800) 245-2737 or (740) 382-3322, www.emusic.com

BOOKS

Books dedicated to home/portable keyboards and digital pianos are very rare, but there are many titles on a wide variety of related subjects, i.e., MIDI, sampling, synthesizers, and music and computers.

INTERNET

The Internet contains vast amounts of information on digital keyboard instruments, MIDI, and related subjects. Below are some relevant websites. Most manufacturers have an informative website too. A glossary of terms is often included.

- Creative Synth: www.creativesynth.com

The information in this section is subject to change and not intended to be complete.

- Digital Hell: techno.king.net/synthetic-fruit/dh
- EEEI Equipment database: industrial.org/gear.php
- Electronic Music Foundation: www.emf.org
- Harmony Central: www.harmonycentral.com
- International Association of Electronic Keyboard Manufacturers: www.iaekm.org
- Loops: www.loops.net
- MIDI.com: www.midi.com
- MIDI Farm: www.midifarm.com
- Midirobot: www.midirobot.com
- Music Machines: machines.hyperreal.org
- Sample Net: www.samplenet.com
- Song Stuff: www.songstuff.com
- Sonic State: www.sonicstate.com
- Sound on Sound: www.soundonsound.com
- Synth Zone: www.synthzone.com
- Synthfool: www.synthfool.com
- Virtual synthesizer museum: www.synthmuseum.com

OTHER TITLES IN THE TIPBOOK SERIES

The Tipbook Series also includes *Tipbook Music on Paper*, which tells you basically everything you need to know about sheet music and music theory: reading notes, dynamic markings, articulation signs, and so on. This book, illustrated with numerous easily playable examples, teaches you to read music in a couple of chapters. It's also a highly accessible reference book, should you need to brush up on transposing, the circle of fifths, scales, and much more. Two more Tipbooks that may be of interest are *Tipbook Piano*, which tells you all the ins and outs on the acoustic instrument, and – scheduled for release in 2004 – *Tipbook Amplifiers & Effects*. Additional and up-to-date information on the Tipbook Series can be found at www.tipbook.com.

ESSENTIAL DATA

In the event of your equipment being stolen or lost, or if you decide to sell it, it's useful to have all relevant data at hand. Here are two pages to makes those notes. For the insurance, for the police, or just for yourself.

INSURANCE

Company:	
Phone:	Fax:
Broker:	
Phone:	Fax:
Email:	Website:
Policy number:	Premium:
Renewal date:	

INSTRUMENTS AND ACCESSORIES

Make and model:	
Serial number:	
Price:	
Date of purchase:	
Dealer:	
Phone:	Fax:
E-mail:	Website:

Make and model:	
Serial number:	
Price:	
Date of purchase:	
Dealer:	
Phone:	Fax:
E-mail:	Website:

ADDITIONAL NOTES

....
....
....
....
....
....
....
....

....
....
....
....
....
....
....
....
....
....
....